The
Parables
of
Mercy

The
Parables
of
Mercy

PONTIFICAL COUNCIL FOR THE PROMOTION
OF THE NEW EVANGELIZATION

Jubilee of Mercy
2015-2016

Our Sunday Visitor Publishing Division
Our Sunday Visitor, Inc.
Huntington, Indiana 46750

Copyright © 2015 Pontifical Council for the Promotion of the New Evangelization
Vatican City

Published 2015 by Our Sunday Visitor Publishing Division

20 19 18 17 16 15   1 2 3 4 5 6 7 8 9

Our Sunday Visitor Publishing Division, Our Sunday Visitor, Inc., 200 Noll Plaza, Huntington, IN 46750; 1-800-348-2440

ISBN: 978-1-61278-977-4 (Inventory No. T1737)
eISBN: 978-1-61278-985-9
LCCN: 2015947541

Translation: Marsha Daigle-Williamson
Cover design: Lindsey Riesen
Cover art: Shutterstock; Pontifical Council for Promotion of the New Evangelization
Interior design: Sherri Hoffman

PRINTED IN THE UNITED STATES OF AMERICA

TABLE OF CONTENTS

PREFACE

In *Misericordiae Vultus* (the papal bull proclaiming the Jubilee Year of Mercy), Pope Francis writes, "With our eyes fixed on Jesus and his merciful gaze, we experience the love of the Most Holy Trinity" (8). The mission Jesus received from the Father is none other than revealing the very love that gives itself to every person without excluding anyone: "Everything in him speaks of mercy. Nothing in him is devoid of compassion" (8). This wonderful saying can serve as an introduction for the reflections in this pastoral book as it lays out *The Parables of Mercy*. It makes for provocative reading. Delving into the parables helps us understand Jesus' teaching in them, but above all it helps us recognize ourselves in the stories. There is probably nothing like the parables to engage readers in the existential dimensions of life that shine through them and to guide readers in making life changes.

Pope Francis also invites us to perceive the overall message contained in the parables when he states, "Jesus reveals the nature of God as that of a Father who never gives up until he has forgiven the wrong and overcome rejection with compassion and mercy. We know these parables well, three in particular: the lost sheep, the lost coin, and the father with two sons (cf. Lk 15:1-32). In these parables, God is always presented as full of joy, especially when he pardons. In them we find the core of the Gospel and of our faith, because mercy is presented as a force that overcomes everything, filling the heart with love and bringing consolation through pardon" (9).

The Pontifical Council for the Promotion of the New Evangelization owes thanks to Monsignor Antonio Pitta for having accepted the invitation to write this commentary. His well-known competence with the Bible and his direct style provide us with a valuable tool for pastoral work. The genuine spiritual insight and remarkable cultural depth found in this commentary will be of assistance in personal reflection, catechesis, and *lectio divina*. Understanding the parables that are addressed to each of us will help us live out the Holy Year of Mercy in a way that witnesses to the faith we profess.

✠ Rino Fisichella
President, Pontifical Council for the
Promotion of the New Evangelization

CHAPTER ONE

Introduction: Jesus, Mercy, and the Parables

"Be merciful, even as your Father is merciful" (Lk 6:36) is one of Jesus' boldest statements. The Jewish people knew the fact that God the Father is merciful, but to think that human beings can be like him raises a problem. Can we ever be as merciful as our Father? And for what reasons should we be like him? The "Gospel of Mercy," which is what Luke's Gospel is called, tells the life of Jesus with mercy as its main theme.

Before even talking about mercy, Jesus made us feel it and see it. One of his first miracles is for a leper: "Moved with pity, he stretched out his hand and touched him" (Mk 1:41). Moved by compassion, Jesus is not afraid of becoming infected. The cry of the blind man in Jericho is louder for Jesus than the cry of those who try to silence him: "Jesus, Son of David, have mercy on me!" (Lk 18:38).

His encounters with the sick and with sinners are full of mercy. Out of compassion he frees a woman who is about to be stoned (see Jn 8:3-11). The way he allows himself to be touched by a sinful woman disgusts Simon the Pharisee (Lk 7:36-50). Jesus does not speak about mercy in the abstract. Rather than defining it, he talks about it through parables. Which parables? Why use parables? For whom is the mercy in these parables, and how is it demonstrated?

9

1. Which Parables Are About Mercy?

For those who are familiar with the Bible, the "parables of mercy" call to mind the three stories in Luke 15:1-32: the lost sheep, the lost coin, and the prodigal son. However, the concept of mercy is also expanded in other parables of Jesus: the two debtors and their creditor (Lk 7:41-43), the good Samaritan (Lk 10:25-37), the rich man and the beggar Lazarus (Lk 16:19-31), the unjust judge and the persistent widow (Lk 18:1-8), and the Pharisee and the publican in the temple (Lk 18:9-14).

In the third Gospel, eight of Jesus' parables deal with mercy from different angles. Seven of them are told during Jesus' journey toward Jerusalem (Lk 9:51—19:46). Only the short parable of the debtors and their creditor (Lk 7:41-43) is told during the time he was still preaching in Galilee. Since for much of that journey in Luke's Gospel Jesus is telling parables of mercy, it is appropriate to examine what he says about the many aspects of mercy.

Mercy is not a natural virtue that depends on a person's character; the most virtuous person is not necessarily more merciful than someone else. Instead mercy is a question of an inner disposition that matures as one spends time with Jesus. That is how we learn mercy! Of course, not all of Jesus' parables concern mercy, and the topic of mercy is not communicated only through parables. The parables, however, deserve to be looked at separately, and the exhortation to "Be merciful, even as your Father is merciful" is the key to accessing them.

2. Why Use Parables?

Why use parables to talk about mercy rather than other ways of communicating about it? And why so many parables on mercy? Why isn't the parable of the prodigal son — or the parable of the merciful father, as people today prefer to call it — enough? Charity and wisdom are praiseworthy, but we should add mercy to that list. If we really think about it, if we are supposed to be merciful like (and because) the Father is merciful, it is impossible to speak about mercy apart from the people who actually have it or are lacking it. If Jesus prefers to tell stories about mercy rather than define it, he has his reasons, which we will try to highlight.

2.1. A Mirror of Life

Jesus' parables, including those on mercy, are linked to real life and depict it. It would be a mistake to think that after having read one of his parables, we need to interpret it. The very opposite is true: the parables interpret people's lives and challenge them!

The parable of the two debtors and the creditor (Lk 7:41-43) is inspired by the embarrassing situation at the home of Simon the Pharisee. Jesus lets his feet be washed and kissed by a sinful woman. The parable he tells in that episode illustrates that the debtor who is forgiven the larger sum of money is more grateful to his creditor than the person who has less debt to repay. If the woman washes Jesus' feet, it is because he has forgiven her sin; it is not the case that she is forgiven because she washed his feet.

The three parables in Luke 15, which are generally known as "the parables of mercy," follow the statement that Jesus is eating with sinners. The parables bring clarity to that situation and force those who criticize Jesus to rethink their judgments. After those three parables, Jesus' remarks about a person who exalts himself before God (see Lk 16:15) lead to his parable of the rich man and the beggar Lazarus. The parable of the judge and the persistent widow (Lk 18:1-8) explains the importance of prayer: if people are persistent, they are capable of changing God's mind. The parable of the Pharisee and the tax collector in the Temple (Lk 18:9-14) arises from the presumption of people who look down on others to exalt themselves.

Jesus mirrors real life in his parables — our relationship with God and with other sinners. For this reason the characters in the parables are anonymous and the locations in which they act are indeterminate. All listeners become part of Jesus' parables and are mirrored there with a disarming truth, causing them to rethink the relationships they participate in every day.

2.2. He, I, and the Other

Real life is conveyed through Jesus' parables, and all the ones about mercy are told in terms of a three-way relationship. For convenience sake, we can refer to it as "he, I, and the other." The scenes involve two debtors and one creditor; a priest, a Levite, and a Samaritan; a shepherd, ninety-nine sheep, and one lost sheep; a housewife, nine drachmas, and one lost drachma; a father of two sons, one of whom was dead and then returned to life; an anonymous rich man, Lazarus, and Abraham; an unjust judge, God, and a widow; a Pharisee, a tax collector, and God in the Temple.

Since we also find parables in the Gospels that focus on one element, like the parable about the mustard seed that grows on its own (see Lk 13:18-19), or on two elements, like the parable of the leaven and the dough (Lk 13:20-21), the threefold relationship in the parables of mercy is intentional. This structure implies a message we cannot overlook. The mercy of God is often linked to the mercy displayed by human beings and does not occur in a vacuum or merely in terms of "my" relationship to God. "Be merciful, even as [and because] your Father is merciful" (Lk 6:36) is the central architectural beam of mercy in parable form.

2.3. The Reversal

The parables of mercy take nothing for granted and have in common a reversal of the situation. They checkmate the listeners because the situations are resolved in surprising ways that are contrary to what would be expected.

In answer to Jesus' question about which of the two debtors would love his creditor more, Simon responds, "The one, I suppose, to whom he forgave more" (Lk 7:43). Without wanting to, he justifies the sinful woman who is washing Jesus' feet. At the end of the parable of the good Samaritan, when Jesus was asked who the neighbor is (see Lk 10:29), the answer obliges the lawyer to make himself everyone's neighbor and to imitate the person who had compassion on the dying man (v. 37). Contrary to normal logic, the shepherd leaves ninety-nine sheep in the desert to go look for the missing one and risks becoming a shepherd who has no flock at all (Lk 15:3-7).

The parable of the merciful father is shocking because he reverses the situation of the sons. For the younger son who asks to be treated like one of the hired servants, the father re-confers the dignity of being a son; however, facing the older son who condemns his brother with his dismissive phrase "this son of yours" (Lk 15:30), the father inverts his phrase with "this your brother" (Lk 15:32). The reversal concerning the rich man and Lazarus is puzzling: The former has enjoyed good things in this life, but the latter is now comforted for all eternity (Lk 16:25). If an unjust judge grants the requests of a widow after a long time, then God immediately grants the requests of his chosen (Lk 18:7-8). The reversal that occurs between the Pharisee and the publican in the Temple is unimaginable: the former prays a long time and lists all his good works but is not justified; the latter recognizes he is a sinner and goes home justified without performing any sacrifice for the expiation of his sins (Lk 18:14).

All of this is upside down, like an inverted pyramid! The parables of mercy catch the hearers off guard because God's action in them reverses every kind of firm certainty people have and forces them to reconsider their way of thinking about God and of envisioning Jesus.

2.4. Mercy Seen from the Inside

The issue of mercy is a heart issue, which should not, however, be confused with sentimentalism. In the Bible, the heart is the seat of thought, the center from which people's most intimate decisions are made. For this reason, "to have compassion" or mercy is the equivalent of an inner visceral impulse that connects someone to the other. If we exclude the shorter parables — the two debtors, the rescued sheep, and the recovered drachma — the turning point in the more fully articulated parables occurs in the human heart.

Compassion for the dying man, which the priest and the Levite do not have, is found in a Samaritan man: "when he saw him, he had compassion" (Lk 10:33). Compassion puts wings on the feet of the merciful father: "While he [the younger son] was yet at a distance, he had compassion" (Lk 15:20). Even though the younger son is suffering from hunger, if he had not come to his senses, he would not have taken the road back home. It is only when the unjust judge talks to himself that he decides to give the widow justice (see Lk 18:4-5). The Pharisee's arrogant prayer is in contrast to the tax collector's prayer, "God, be merciful to me a sinner!" (Lk 18:13).

The beauty in the parables of mercy is reflected in a human heart laid bare and is uncovered in the depth of compassion demonstrated toward one's neighbor. Since it is poles apart from cheap mercy, it is a mercy that generates passion among human beings and can be compared to God's. There is no mercy when people lack the willingness to look within themselves; all that remains is the luxury of a rich man, clothed in purple and expensive linen but incapable of seeing poor Lazarus who lies neglected in front of the large entrance to his house (see Lk 16:19-20)!

3. For Whom Are the Parables of Mercy?

God's mercy is for everyone, but it is also for very specific people. The parables involve two categories of people: those in the parables and those who hear them.

The parable of the two debtors pardoned by their creditor, for example, also involves Jesus, Simon, and the sinful woman because of the context in which it is told! If at the beginning of the parable of the good Samaritan the dying man is the object of compassion, in the end the neighbor is the very Samaritan himself, so the lawyer is being exhorted to become a neighbor to the other. Sinners correspond to the lost sheep and the missing drachma while the Pharisees and scribes seem to share the lot of the ninety-nine sheep left in the desert and the nine drachmas that are still safe and secure (but not really!). The parable of the merciful father is filled with the father's compassion for one son and his entreaty of the other son. This time it is not so easy to convince the Pharisees and the scribes about mercy, since the sons are not as innocent as the sheep and the coin.

The poor man Lazarus is carried by angels to Abraham's bosom, but the rich man is not granted any of his requests. People who are attached to money should not deceive themselves that their opulent lifestyle continues into the afterlife. If the widow is the recipient of mercy the unjust judge grants her, how much more does God listen to his chosen ones. A tax collector who admits he is a sinner is justified, but not the Pharisee who exalts himself. Whoever exalts himself by scorning others has something to think about in the face of such a scathing parable.

The range of sinners in the parables is not dictated by populism or to imply a social revolution, but is presented because Jesus wants to implicate all his listeners. Otherwise, it might be easy to have mercy for only a few people if mercy is in fact based on merit and not grace.

The bridge tying the first and the last parable of mercy together is notable. The first parable is told in the house of Simon the Pharisee when a sinner washes Jesus' feet (see Lk 7:41-43), and the last parable presents a Pharisee and a tax collector who realizes he is a sinner (Lk 18:9-14). The parables of mercy do not leave people untouched; they involve the listeners profoundly and bring them into the story.

CHAPTER TWO

Whoever Is Forgiven More Loves More

The Two Debtors and the Creditor
Luke 7:36-50

The short parable told in Luke 7:41-43 sheds light on distinct situations in Jesus' public life. He visits with sinful men and women and even assumes to himself the right to forgive their sins. This is a prerogative that, for the Jews of that time, belongs only to God and is regulated by the priests in the Temple. This parable is told while Jesus is at dinner in the house of Simon the Pharisee. Because of its beauty the parable deserves to be seen in the context in which it is told:

> One of the Pharisees asked him to eat with him, and he went into the Pharisee's house, and sat at table. And behold, a woman of the city, who was a sinner, when she learned that he was sitting at table in the Pharisee's house, brought an alabaster flask of ointment, and standing behind him at his feet, weeping, she began to wet his feet with her tears, and wiped them with the hair of her head, and kissed his feet, and anointed them

with the ointment. Now when the Pharisee who had invited him saw it, he said to himself, "If this man were a prophet, he would have known who and what sort of woman this is who is touching him, for she is a sinner." And Jesus answering said to him, "Simon, I have something to say to you." And he answered, "What is it, Teacher?" "A certain creditor had two debtors; one owed five hundred denarii, and the other fifty. When they could not pay, he forgave them both. Now which of them will love him more?" Simon answered, "The one, I suppose, to whom he forgave more." And he said to him, "You have judged rightly." Then turning toward the woman he said to Simon, "Do you see this woman? I entered your house, you gave me no water for my feet, but she has wet my feet with her tears and wiped them with her hair. You gave me no kiss, but from the time I came in she has not ceased to kiss my feet. You did not anoint my head with oil, but she has anointed my feet with ointment. Therefore I tell you, her sins, which are many, are forgiven, for she loved much; but he who is forgiven little, loves little." And he said to her, "Your sins are forgiven." Then those who were at table with him began to say among themselves, "Who is this, who even forgives sins?" And he said to the woman, "Your faith has saved you; go in peace." (Lk 7:36-50)

1. Embarrassing Love

The hospitality that Jesus receives in the house of Simon the Pharisee is one of embarrassing intimacy. The event involves an ordinary dinner invitation Jesus willingly accepts. During the meal a woman arrives who is known in that area for her bad reputation. Without having been invited or having asked permission from anyone, she approaches Jesus, bathes his feet with her tears, wipes them with her hair, kisses his feet, and pours perfume over them. Her actions are shocking because she is a sinner, and Simon immediately labeled her as such. Nevertheless, Simon's attention is not focused on the sinner but on Jesus. How can someone who is considered a prophet let his feet be washed this way? Therefore, the person under judgment here is not the woman, quickly assessed as a sinner, but Jesus, who is defiled by her sin because he let her touch him.

The sinful woman performs certain actions that bewilder Simon and his other guests. With her hands, her tears, and her hair, she defiles Jesus. How can someone ever communicate such a scandalous gospel? Only a parable can help us understand why Jesus is provoking such a scandal!

2. The Two Debtors and Their Creditor

Jesus' passion for sinners is very humane and gratuitous, without any ulterior motive. This short parable clarifies what is occurring in Simon's house. As short as it is, it is nevertheless incisive and hits the mark well! Not to reveal the implication of the parable as it relates to the current situation all at once, he tells the story of the two debtors and their creditor. As usual, Jesus does not name these people but focuses on the central issue of the story. The creditor is owed five hundred denarii by the first debtor and fifty by the other. The disproportion is noteworthy because the fifty denarii owed by the second debtor are multiplied by ten for the first debtor. To put this in context, fifty denarii would represent about two months' worth of work while five hundred would be the equivalent of two and a half years of earned income.

Jesus makes clear that the two debtors cannot repay the sums they owe and are pardoned by their creditor. The characters in the parable do not speak; there is no dialogue between the debtors and their creditor. All the attention is on the word "forgave," which indicates the pardon for the debtors. And it is the creditor's gracious pardon that generates Jesus' question to Simon about which debtor will love the creditor more.

Simon is still not aware that he is a party in the case and answers that the debtor who had more debt canceled would love the creditor more. His answer unmasks him and incriminates him! Had he been more attentive to the parable, he would have remembered that since any kind of sin is a debt that has been incurred, only grace can make up for the debt everyone owes God. Simon clearly seems unable to overcome the emotional shock of the grace that Jesus grants the sinful woman.

3. "He Who Is Forgiven Little, Loves Little" (v. 47)

The parable moves off center stage for Jesus to reveal the actual situation: Simon is like the debtor who owes two months' pay, and for that reason did not give Jesus any water for his feet, or greet him with a kiss, or anoint his head. The sinful woman is like the debtor who owed two and a half years of salary: She would never succeed in paying off the debt. The only way out for both of them is grace! The parable's major impact on the situation concerns the relationship between the remission of sins and the love of the sinful woman. Unfortunately, some translations render the sentence in verse 47 as "her sins are forgiven *because* she has loved much." However, the original Greek expresses the consequences of the forgiveness of sin: "her sins are forgiven, and *therefore* she has loved much." If such great guilt had not been forgiven, she would not have been so disposed to love. The woman is able to love because she has been given unconditional grace.

The second part of Jesus' answer confirms the primacy of grace: "He who is forgiven little, loves little" (v. 47). This assertion links the parable to real life: whoever has not been reached by God's freely given love is not in a position to love him.

4. The Remission of Sins and the Faith That Saves

During this meal, Jesus scandalizes all the guests who murmur among themselves, "Who is this, who even forgives sins?" (v. 49). The question calls for the most logical answer, which is that only God can forgive sins (see Lk 5:21). And while God can forgive sins, it is obligatory to expiate them according to the law. Jesus is appropriating a divine, not a human, right to himself; so this is an abuse on his part in the guests' minds.

Nevertheless, this very "abuse" bridges the gap between the parable and the encounter in Simon's house. With the power to forgive the sins of a sinful woman, Jesus is in tune with God's way of acting. He forgives her because he recognizes the faith the sinful woman had right from the beginning in his power to forgive sins. If, on hearing Jesus was at Simon's house, she ran to buy costly perfume and overcame whatever obstacle there was to seeing him, it is because she has an unshakeable confidence that Jesus is able to forgive sins (like the creditor who forgave the one who owed 500 denarii).

Faith is the only condition that Jesus asks of someone to be saved; it is even the common denominator in all his miracles. In this regard, there is a similarity between forgiving the sins of a sinful woman and the healing of a paralytic or a blind man: in the healing events as well, it is *faith that saves*, not the miracle itself.

5. What Is the Implication for the Community?

Let us look at the parable of the merciful king in Matthew 18:23-35. As in the parable in Luke 7:41-43, there is a creditor (the king) and two debtors (servants). The first servant owes ten thousand talents to the king, but his pleading arouses the compassion of the king who forgives him his debt. Unfortunately, the servant hardly leaves the palace when he meets another servant who owes him one hundred denarii; he deals with him harshly and has him thrown into prison.

The disproportion of the debts is incalculable. If in Jesus' time one talent was the equivalent of ten thousand denarii, then ten thousand talents is an inconceivable sum with respect to one hundred denarii owed by the second servant. Practically speaking, the second servant could have discharged his debt with less than six months of work while the first servant could never have repaid his debt to the king. The grace the first servant received from the king was wasted! The king, informed of what happened to the other servant, condemns him: "'You wicked servant! I forgave you all that debt because you pleaded with me; and should not you have had mercy on your fellow servant, as I had mercy on you?'" (Mt 18:32-33). So the servant is turned over to the jailers until he can repay a debt that is impossible to pay even if he worked for the rest of his life. The conclusion of the parable is dramatic: "So also my heavenly Father will do to every one of you, if you do not forgive your brother from your heart" (Mt 18:35).

The Church consists of servants to whom an immeasurable debt has been forgiven so that they are able to forgive other servants. What if a Church, having been commanded to forgive seventy times seven, or forever (see Mt 18:21-22), placed conditions on the mercy of God? Would it be capable of recognizing that God's mercy is greater than any human sin? And that mercy should never be considered a right for some but only something possibly granted to others?

With Jesus, God's mercy allows itself to be contaminated by human misery, but he redeems that misery by transforming it through gratuitous unconditional love. There is no episode in the Gospels that is more intimate than this one in Simon's house. A sinful woman touches Jesus' feet, washes them with her tears, wipes them with her hair, and kisses him with her lips. According to the Gospels, Jesus never conceded this intimacy to anyone, not even his mother. Jesus' mercy redeems human misery not by merely brushing up against it or barely touching it but by letting himself be contaminated by it.

CHAPTER THREE

Compassion for a Stranger

The Good Samaritan
Luke 10:25-37

The parable of the good Samaritan is one of Jesus' most provocative parables. He had just set out on his journey to Jerusalem with his disciples. He encounters a lawyer with whom he dialogues about how to inherit eternal life. The lawyer is trying to test him on one of the most debated questions of the day: What is the most important commandment of the Law on which eternal life depends? The situation inspires the parable of the good Samaritan, which unravels the intricate relationship between the Law and its central core:

> And behold, a lawyer stood up to put him to the test, saying, "Teacher, what shall I do to inherit eternal life?" He said to him, "What is written in the law? What do you read there?" And he answered, "You shall love the Lord your God with all your heart, and with all your soul, and with all your strength, and with all your mind; and your neighbor as yourself." And he said to him, "You have answered right; do this, and you will live."
>
> But he, desiring to justify himself, said to Jesus, "And who is my neighbor?" Jesus replied, "A man was going

23

down from Jerusalem to Jericho, and he fell among robbers, who stripped him and beat him, and departed,
leaving him half dead. Now by chance a priest was going
down that road; and when he saw him he passed by on
the other side. So likewise a Levite, when he came to
the place and saw him, passed by on the other side. But
a Samaritan, as he journeyed, came to where he was;
and when he saw him, he had compassion, and went to
him and bound up his wounds, pouring on oil and wine;
then he set him on his own beast and brought him to
an inn, and took care of him. And the next day he took
out two denarii and gave them to the innkeeper, saying,
'Take care of him; and whatever more you spend, I will
repay you when I come back.' Which of these three, do
you think, proved neighbor to the man who fell among
the robbers?" He said, "The one who showed mercy on
him." And Jesus said to him, "Go and do likewise." (Lk
10:25-37)

1. The Most Important Commandment

In the Palestine of Jesus' time, it seems there was a debate
among the various religious groups on two key questions about the
Law of Moses: Which commandment is the most important? And
who is the neighbor people are called to love? The multiplication
of laws made it necessary to come to an essential synthesis of the
Law to discover its core. On the other side of the scale, with politi-
cal tensions among the various groups including the Samaritans,
people were asking who was defined as their neighbor. Was it only
people who belonged to their own religious group, or was it also
people who shared a faith in one God, including even a Samaritan?
Although the lawyer's second question is loaded because he is trying
to have Jesus fall into a trap, it does reflect how much this issue was
being debated by the different groups in Palestine.

The first part of the dialogue takes on the first question. In terms of the multiplication of laws, the lawyer and Jesus both agree that love for God and for neighbor are the necessary conditions for inheriting eternal life. The lawyer, in his answer, refers to passages in Deuteronomy 6:5 and in Leviticus 19:18 to link love for God with love for neighbor.

At this point the lawyer lays a more insidious trap: Who is the neighbor people should love? A brother, an acquaintance, a friend, a stranger, or even an enemy? Can people consider someone who ignores love for God as their neighbor? In his teaching strategy in this parable, Jesus combines the two major commandments by speaking of love of neighbor in a way that implies love for God without speaking of it directly.

2. The Priest, the Levite, and the Samaritan

As usual, the people in the parable are anonymous, but Jesus does focus attention on their religious and ethnic identities. Jesus starts the story off in a distant location. He has not yet reached Jericho in his journey toward Jerusalem, and he speaks about a man who "was going down" from the holy city to Jericho. The road connecting the two cities was more than sixteen miles long and was dangerous because it crossed the Wadi Qelt.[1] While Jerusalem is at 2,461 feet above sea level, Jericho is about 1,312 feet below sea level, so it is necessary to "go down" from Jerusalem to reach Jericho, just as the parable recounts. Jesus says that some bandits rob a man and leave him half dead. The dying man's condition is the sensitive issue in the parable. Can someone be in contact with a dying man without risking defilement?

It is not by chance that the three people who are selected in the parable are involved in the worship of the one God in various ways: a priest who is coming down from Jerusalem after performing his Temple service; a Levite who belongs to the priestly class but does

---

1. Wadi Qelt is a valley that runs west to east across the Judean Desert; it originates near Jerusalem and ends near Jericho.

not perform Temple service; and a Samaritan. And here things start not to add up because the normal triad should include a priest, a Levite, and an *Israelite* (see Dt 18:1; 27:9). The Samaritan is the odd man in the triad because, according to Jewish thinking, he is unclean and is considered a foreigner. The main reason for the friction between the two nations emerges in the dialogue Jesus has with the Samaritan woman. On which mountain should people worship God? On the mount in Jerusalem or on Mount Gerizim where the Samaritans worship (see Jn 4:20)?

According to Mosaic Law, whoever touches a cadaver is unclean for a week. If someone becomes contaminated and then performs a ritual action, he is to be excluded from Israel (see Nm 19:11-13). The rule applies even more so for a priest and even in the case of one of his relatives who has died (Lv 21:1-4). So this situation involves pre-existing boundaries. The priest and the Levite are faced with the alternative of observing the laws of ritual purity or of helping a dying man. However, it is good to point out that cultural norms do not excuse the priest or the Levite, because in a situation like the one in the parable they are also obligated to help the dying man. Instead, both of them see him and pass by.

Finally, a Samaritan sees the dying man. He feels compassion for him and takes care of him. So the parable creates an untenable contrast: what the priest and the Levite avoid doing is done by a Samaritan, who is an enemy. The content of the parable begins to be provocative since love for God does not automatically guarantee love for neighbor. In addition, what would be expected from those who know more about the love of God (the priest and the Levite) is accomplished by someone who is defined only by his ethnic difference. The dying man is rescued by a foreigner!

3. From Compassion to Care

The parable reaches its turning point when it states that the Samaritan "had compassion" (v. 33) on the dying man, so at the end the lawyer recognizes that the neighbor is "the one who showed mercy on him" (v. 37). It is worth noting here that the verb expressing the Samaritan's compassion, *splanchnizomai* ("have compassion"), derives from the noun *splanchna*, which in Greek means "bowels," including the heart. According to the common way of thinking in Jesus' time, a person's sentiments (love, compassion, mercy) are expressed viscerally: The Samaritan does not stop at merely seeing the dying man but becomes involved in his innermost self, and it is such visceral compassion that sets in motion the possibility of saving the dying man.

True compassion is not a feeling but an action that results in caring for the other. Jesus recounts the help the Samaritan gives the dying man with attention to the specific details: he approaches him, he cleans him up, he binds up his wounds, he sets him on his mount, he takes him to the inn, and he takes cares of him there. After the man lives through the first night (when there is the most risk of his dying), the Samaritan then gives the innkeeper two denarii, the equivalent of two days' wages. When he leaves to continue his journey, he guarantees the innkeeper that if there are other expenses, he will repay him on his return.

From beginning to end, there are no details about the dying man. He is not described in terms of his origins or his social status. All the attention is on who is taking care of him and paying for him. True compassion leads a person to become involved in doing good and to succeed, despite the cost of time and money, on behalf of the one who is helped. St. Ambrose of Milan says it well: "Mercy, not kinship, makes someone a neighbor" (*Exposition of the Gospel of Luke*, 7, 84).

4. The Reversal

Jesus responds to the lawyer's question with the parable of the good Samaritan. The parable sheds light on life by overturning a common way of thinking. In terms of the debates that were current in Jesus' time, we noted that the one concerning the identity of the neighbor was among the most heated. Every group had a different way of understanding who the neighbor was supposed to be. Jesus offers the most original response because of what he recounts in the parable; he turns the debate upside down.

If at the beginning the neighbor is the dying man, in the end he is the Samaritan. The dying man is the answer to the lawyer's question ("Who is my neighbor?"), but the Samaritan is the answer to Jesus' question, "Which of these three, do you think, proved neighbor to the man?" The lawyer still does not realize that he is about to become a party to the case. He recognizes, with searing truth, that the neighbor is no longer the dying man but the one who had compassion on him. He is thus forced to give an answer that he does not want to give: the neighbor is the Samaritan — whom the lawyer only refers to as "the one who . . ." rather than referring to his ethnic identity.

Jesus reveals to the lawyer how the parable connects to life. He exhorts him to enter into the logic of the parable — like a reader entering into a story — and to act like the Samaritan by making *himself* the neighbor of another. Based on the first question in the dialogue about the greatest commandment, the question about who the neighbor is leads to a debate that has no resolution until people can point to themselves. The parable transforms the common mode of thinking about who the neighbor is by requiring the hearers to start with themselves. A neighbor is not to be defined by religious, cultural, or social origins, but by compassion for the other.

5. Jesus, the Good Samaritan?

Since the time of the Fathers of the Church, this parable has been read as depicting Jesus' human traits. Clement of Alexandria comments: "Who more than he [Jesus] has pitied us, who by the rulers of darkness were all but put to death with many wounds, fears, lusts, passions, pains deceits, pleasures? Of these wounds the only physician is Jesus, who cuts out the passions thoroughly by the root" (*Who Is the Rich Man That Shall Be Saved?*, 29).

Different details of the parable can make us think of Jesus who, among other things, stopped to dialogue with a Samaritan woman (see Jn 4:7ff). Such deep compassion that is capable of transforming itself into caring for the sick is typical of Jesus. Even the secondary details, like that of the good Samaritan leaving the inn and returning later, can made us think of a parallel with Jesus leaving after his resurrection and returning at his second coming.

Nevertheless, interpreting the parable as referring only to Jesus would impoverish it. What is said of the Samaritan applies to Jesus *and* to the Christian community, where dedication to one's neighbor is transformed into attentive care for whatever person is recognized as "the other." Therefore, the parable portrays everyone's daily life and transforms it from within: it clarifies for the lawyer that love for God cannot be separated from love for neighbor.

6. The Fulfillment of the Law

The early Christian communities followed the trajectory of Jesus' path and deepened the significance of the parable of the good Samaritan. On two occasions St. Paul refers to the debate about the most important commandment in the Law. He says to the Galatians who risk devouring each other, "The whole law is fulfilled in one word, 'You shall love your neighbor as yourself'" (Gal 5:14). Christian freedom is absolute because it is a gift from Christ: "For freedom Christ has set us free" (Gal 5:1). This is the reason such freedom should not lead to anarchy but should incarnate itself in service and love for one's neighbor. When Paul then addresses the Christians in Rome, he returns to the commandment of love and considers it the unique debt that believers should have, since to some extent people are always lacking in love (see Rom 13:9). On both occasions Paul does not mention love for God but focuses his attention on love for one's neighbor. Why does there seem to be such a clear imbalance and silence about love for God?

The reason is given in the First Letter of John: "He who does not love his brother whom he has seen, cannot love God whom he has not seen" (4:20). The great risk that Paul and John foresee is that in the name of love for God serious abuses and omissions could occur in the Church. People's perception of their own love for God is easy to tailor to their own standards and needs, but it is a different matter when it comes to actually loving a flesh-and-blood neighbor. Love for God does not automatically produce love for a neighbor in all cases, but it is true that love for one's neighbor is a mirror of love for God.

Nevertheless, so as not to delude ourselves, it is helpful to go back to the source, which is the love God has for us. St. John specifies, "We love, because he first loved us" (1 Jn 4:19). To the extent that we have received the love of God, to that extent we are in a position to love our neighbor. Genuine love of neighbor does not come from social projects or simple altruism; rather it comes from the love that God and Jesus Christ have for human beings, and that love in turn evokes the fervor leading people to "live no longer for themselves but for him who for their sake died and was raised" (2 Cor 5:15).

The parable of the good Samaritan gives meaning to human life. We become a neighbor to the other ultimately because God drew near to us and continues, through Christ, to be concerned about our human wounds. That kind of reversal draws the lawyer in and obliges him to change his mind. It is not a question of choosing between love for God and love for our neighbor, but of recognizing that people who love a brother or sister they see also love God whom they do not see. However, it is a bitter reality of human life that the reverse is not always the case: love of God does not automatically imply love of neighbor. Love for God, however, is always operative in love for the other.

CHAPTER FOUR

Finding the Lost Sheep and Lost Coin

Luke 15:1-10

The fifteenth chapter of Luke's Gospel is among the most beautiful in the New Testament. What is on display is the compassion of Jesus Christ for sinners as demonstrated by the three parables in this chapter. Generally known as the "parables of mercy," these parables — the lost sheep, the lost coin, and the compassionate father — follow each other without interruption. However, it is appropriate to distinguish the first two from the third because the third is much more developed insofar as it has different potential endings. In addition, while the first two parables end with a celebration, the third leaves us holding our breath. We are not told if the older brother decides to participate in the feast for the return of the younger brother or if he goes on his way.

> Now the tax collectors and sinners were all drawing near to hear him. And the Pharisees and the scribes murmured, saying, "This man receives sinners and eats with them."
>
> So he told them this parable: "What man of you, having a hundred sheep, if he has lost one of them, does

not leave the ninety-nine in the wilderness, and go after the one which is lost, until he finds it? And when he has found it, he lays it on his shoulders, rejoicing. And when he comes home, he calls together his friends and his neighbors, saying to them, 'Rejoice with me, for I have found my sheep which was lost.' Just so, I tell you, there will be more joy in heaven over one sinner who repents than over ninety-nine righteous persons who need no repentance.

Or what woman, having ten silver coins, if she loses one coin, does not light a lamp and sweep the house and seek diligently until she finds it? And when she has found it, she calls together her friends and neighbors, saying, 'Rejoice with me, for I have found the coin which I had lost.' Just so, I tell you, there is joy before the angels of God over one sinner who repents." (Lk 15:1-10)

1. The Different Categories of Sinners

In Jesus' time four categories of sinners could be distinguished, so the conventional thinking went, according to physical, racial, social, and moral characteristics. It appears that Jesus had relationships with people in all four categories.

The first category of sinners can be referred to as "physical" due to the concept that any physical handicap is linked to sin. Sicknesses were seen as consequences of sin and not as natural conditions. When Jesus heals a man who was blind from birth, his disciples ask him if the blindness is due to the blind man's sin or to the sin of his parents (see Jn 9:1-2). In addition to the idea of a connection between sin and sickness, the idea was widespread in the Palestinian population at the time that only God could remit sin, so whatever miracle occurred had to be compensated for with purification in the Temple. Jesus claims the right to cleanse from sin, as in the case of the paralytic who is lowered through the roof (Mk 2:3-12). His forgiving of sin is seen as a blasphemy that scandalizes those present.

The second category of sinners was based on race. Foreigners were considered sinners because they did not observe the Law according to Jewish traditions. The Samaritan and the Gentiles living in Palestine belong in this category. Submission to the Law of Moses allowed them to be freed from that kind of sin. On the basis of race, Gentiles were not allowed to enter the temple in Jerusalem and were obligated to respect its holy boundaries under pain of stoning if they defiled the sacred place.

In addition to a racial significance for the word "sinner," there was a social significance that applied to the tax collectors, or publicans, who contracted to collect the taxes owed to the imperial power. Unlike moneylenders, the publicans made their living by extorting more money than was owed and keeping the difference. Among his disciples Jesus chooses Levi, son of Alphaeus, whom he invites to follow him while he is working at the tax office (see Mk 2:14). To underscore the restoration of this group of sinners, Jesus tells the parable of the tax collector and the Pharisee in the Temple (Lk 18:9-14), which will be discussed later.

The last category of sinners was moral and included usurers and prostitutes. It is assumed that the woman who washes Jesus' feet in Simon's house is that kind of a sinner. Another example would be the Samaritan woman Jesus stops to speak to at the well who has had five husbands and lives with a man who is not her husband (see Jn 4:7-30).

Jesus maintains he is sent to heal the wounds of all sinners, and no one is excluded. Because of the people he spends time with, however, he is accused of being a sinner himself (see Jn 9:24). But his miracles prove that accusation false since a sinner cannot perform the miracles he does. The parables help explain the reasons that lead him to be with sinners.

2. The Shepherd and the Rescued Sheep

Jesus is not the first to speak about the relationship between the shepherd and the sheep and use it as a metaphor. The prophet

Ezekiel tells a lengthy parable against the shepherds of Israel that could have inspired Jesus' parable: "I myself will be the shepherd of my sheep, and I will make them lie down, says the Lord GOD. I will seek the lost, and I will bring back the strayed, and I will bind up the crippled, and I will strengthen the weak, and the fat and the strong I will watch over; I will feed them in justice" (Ez 34:15-16).

Nevertheless, Jesus' parable is paradoxical! We see a shepherd with a hundred sheep who has lost one. He leaves the rest of the ninety-nine sheep in the desert and goes in search of the missing sheep. Once he finds it, he puts it on his shoulders, goes home, calls his friends together, and asks them to rejoice with him. The paradox is found in the question that Jesus asks to describe the shepherd's choice. In terms of who would make such a choice, no one would really leave ninety-nine sheep in the desert to look for a missing one because he would risk losing the ninety-nine in the desert without any assurance of finding the missing one.

The paradoxical manner in which the shepherd acts explains Jesus' approach: those who think (or assume) they are without sin are like the ninety-nine sheep left alone by themselves without a shepherd. There is a risk for the ninety-nine sheep in the desert as well as for the missing sheep but with the substantial difference that the lost sheep needs to be rescued while the others might think they are safe.

The joy at the end of the parable is true to life. Finding a lost sheep is the joy of a shepherd . . . and of God who rejoices more over a converted sinner than over ninety-nine righteous people who do not (or deceive themselves that they do not) need conversion. The way Jesus sees conversion is thought-provoking: it is not the fruit of the one who converts but the fruit of the action of God who seeks the one who is lost. Conversion is always the action of grace given by the One who puts the lost sheep on his shoulders and goes home. And since conversion originates from grace, it needs to be shared. The Pharisees and the scribes have a choice. They can share the joy of conversion given to publicans and sinners, or they can object to it, falling into the presumption of being safe in the desert, like a flock that is actually in harm's way because it has no shepherd.

The human component of conversion is important, especially since people are not compliant like sheep. Nevertheless, the parable is not presenting a moral either about the ninety-nine sheep or the rescued sheep. In other words, a person does not need to be lost in order to be found; nor does being left in the desert mean a person is not being sought by God. All the actions are on the part of the shepherd, not the sheep. The parable of the drachma is added next to highlight the divine origin of conversion.

3. The Housewife and the Recovered Drachma

A housewife who loses a drachma and does everything she can to find it makes the situation of the shepherd and his sheep that is somewhat hard to imagine more plausible. Once the coin is found the woman gathers her friends and neighbors and asks them to rejoice with her because she has found the lost coin. The conclusion of the parable is analogous to the one about the lost sheep: there is joy before the angels of God for a single sinner who repents. On a first reading, it seems that the content of the two parables are very similar. The hundred sheep correspond to the ten coins, while the lost sheep parallels the lost coin. But the attention in this parable is actually focused on the commitment of the woman to find the lost coin that is worth much less than a sheep. In Jesus' time a drachma was worth about one denarii, one day's worth of work.

Despite the minimal value of the coin, the housewife commits herself wholeheartedly to finding it. The parable does not specify the social status of the woman, but in this case poverty could explain such intense effort at finding the missing coin. Instead the focus is on her meticulous search for the lost coin and the shared joy in finding it. Her dedication and joy, and not the nominal value of the coin, is what actually confers real value on the coin.

A coin is inanimate, which underscores even more that conversion is not conceived of as a human response but as an action of grace by God. This short parable of mercy does not link the lost coin to the other coins, unlike the lost sheep that has a connection to the ninety-nine. The housewife searches for the individual coin because of the value it has for her and not because it is similar to the other drachmas. If there were only one sinner, it would be worth the trouble to look for it, find it, and rejoice.

4. Jesus and the Community with a Shepherd's Face

In terms of the shepherd and the sheep, new facets of that relationship occur in the Gospels of John and Matthew. In John 10:1-16, Jesus talks about his similarity to the good shepherd — which can also be translated as the "beautiful" shepherd — with whom he identifies. He is the good shepherd because he knows his sheep by name and gives his life for them. In caring for the sheep, the shepherd is unlike hirelings and thieves. While the hireling is interested in his own earnings, the shepherd gives himself for the sheep without counting the cost or the time necessary for them to become familiar with him. And while the thief steals the sheep, the shepherd lives for and gives himself for the sheep.

What distinguishes the hireling and the thief from the shepherd is the danger involved. When he sees a wolf, the hireling abandons the sheep and flees because he is not interested in the sheep. A genuine shepherd is identified not merely by the job he is performing but by facing its challenges and dangers — for example, when he needs to decide whether to flee to save his own skin or to stay and lose his life for his sheep. In this total gift of self to the point of death, Jesus is the good (beautiful) shepherd. It is a beauty that derives not from the way he looks but from remaining with his sheep in times of danger.

In his discourse on the good shepherd, Jesus is unique in giving himself to the point of shedding blood, but the Jesus of the Gospel of Matthew adds a new dimension to the relationship between the shepherd and the sheep. Matthew 18:12-14 tells the same parable as the one in Luke 15:3-7, but the context is different because it is a discourse about the Church. The first part is dedicated to the "little ones" the Christian community needs to welcome and ends with the parable of the good shepherd. The different context here focuses attention on the thrust of the parable: "So it is not the will of my Father who is in heaven that one of these little ones should perish" (Mt 18:14). The Church is personally involved in this parable because it is entrusted with the will of the Father not to let any of these little ones be lost.

The Church becomes like the merciful heavenly Father when it acts as a mother in search of a lost sheep: it does not forget the ninety-nine on the mountains but rejoices for the one that is recovered. It is easy to see how the parable of the good shepherd involves the Church and its shepherds. The little ones who cannot find a place in society acquire the right of citizenship in the Christian community. They are not only welcomed but are also sought even when there is the risk of not finding them. Jesus implies a contrast between a Church that embarks only on a path of moralism or efficiency and a Church that places the little ones at the center. If the Church exists wherever two or three are gathered in the name of Jesus, the face of Christ in the Church is the face of these little ones.

Alessandro Manzoni has brilliantly rewritten the parable of the rescued sheep when he tells of the encounters of the character called Unknown with Lucy and Cardinal Frederick Borromeo. We cannot dwell here on Chapters 21 and 23 of *The Betrothed*,[2] but they are recommended for their beauty. Let us only say the chapters revolve around what Lucy says when she encounters the man Unknown: "God pardons so many deeds for one act of mercy!"[3] Her statement prevents the Unknown from committing suicide during an anguished night, and the next day he meets with Cardinal Borromeo. The cardinal in turn recognizes his own guilt and reproaches

---

2. A historical novel first published in 1827 (*I promessi sposi*), this is perhaps the most widely known Italian novel.
3. Alessandro Manzoni, *The Betrothed* (CreateSpace Independent Publishing Platform, 2013), p. 105.

himself for not having looked for Unknown and waiting for him to come visit. And this is Manzoni's recasting of the parable in the words of the cardinal: "We will leave the ninety and nine sheep alone. . . . They are in safety on the mountains. I must now remain with the one which was lost. These people [waiting for the bishop] are perhaps now more satisfied than if they had the poor bishop with them; perhaps God, who has visited you with the wonders and riches of his grace, may even now be filling their hearts with a joy, of which they divine not the cause."[4]

---

4. Ibid., p. 113.

CHAPTER FIVE

Extreme Compassion

The Merciful Father
Luke 15:11-32

With all due respect for the first two parables of mercy, a human being is different from a sheep and even more so from a coin! Jesus, very conscious of that enormous difference, brings in a story now that is a work of art. This is a parable par excellence for good reason, provided, however, that we change the title: it should not be "the prodigal son" or "the good father" but the "merciful or compassionate father." Let us reread the parable in all its richness and profundity:

> And he said, "There was a man who had two sons; and the younger of them said to his father, 'Father, give me the share of property that falls to me.' And he divided his living between them. Not many days later, the younger son gathered all he had and took his journey into a far country, and there he squandered his property in loose living. And when he had spent everything, a great famine arose in that country, and he began to be in want. So he went and joined himself to one of the citizens of that country, who sent him into his fields to feed swine. And

he would gladly have fed on the pods that the swine ate; and no one gave him anything. But when he came to himself he said, 'How many of my father's hired servants have bread enough and to spare, but I perish here with hunger! I will arise and go to my father, and I will say to him, "Father, I have sinned against heaven and before you; I am no longer worthy to be called your son; treat me as one of your hired servants."' And he arose and came to his father. But while he was yet at a distance, his father saw him and had compassion, and ran and embraced him and kissed him. And the son said to him, 'Father, I have sinned against heaven and before you; I am no longer worthy to be called your son.' But the father said to his servants, 'Bring quickly the best robe, and put it on him; and put a ring on his hand, and shoes on his feet; and bring the fatted calf and kill it, and let us eat and make merry; for this my son was dead, and is alive again; he was lost, and is found.' And they began to make merry.

"Now his elder son was in the field; and as he came and drew near to the house, he heard music and dancing. And he called one of the servants and asked what this meant. And he said to him, 'Your brother has come, and your father has killed the fatted calf, because he has received him safe and sound.' But he was angry and refused to go in. His father came out and entreated him, but he answered his father, 'Behold, these many years I have served you, and I never disobeyed your command; yet you never gave me a kid, that I might make merry with my friends. But when this son of yours came, who has devoured your living with harlots, you killed for him the fatted calf!' And he said to him, 'Son, you are always with me, and all that is mine is yours. It was fitting to make merry and be glad, for this your brother was dead, and is alive; he was lost, and is found.'" (Lk 15:11-31)

1. Going Beyond a Just Recompense

The parable of the merciful father is an intricate knot that can be untied by choosing one of the various threads in the story. Let us choose what seems to be the most important thread below the surface: receiving a just recompense.

From the very beginning, Jesus indicates the theme of receiving fair remuneration that is part of the most basic human rights. A man has two sons; one of them asks how much inheritance he is entitled to, and the father divides his goods. In Jesus' time the Jewish law provided that the firstborn would receive two-thirds while the younger would receive one-third of an inheritance (see Dt 21:17). Without putting up any resistance, the father hands over the portion claimed by the younger son. While the younger son squanders his inheritance living in dissolution in a faraway region, the other part of the inheritance is safe and is managed by the older son. According to a fair and just way of thinking, if and when the younger son would return home, he should have nothing to claim from his father and his older brother. Any serious wrongdoing by the younger son could at most be forgiven, but not forgotten! In case the father might forget the unfortunate deviation by the younger son, the older brother will always be ready to remember it for both of them. The law of remuneration would thus be respected: a good recompense for the one who does good, and no recompense (or even punishment) for the one who does wrong.

The parable actually violates the law of just recompense from top to bottom, revealing the extreme love of the father. The father does not stay in the house while he waits for his two sons, he does not verify that the younger son is really repentant, and he does not ask where his part of the inheritance ended up. Instead he organizes a feast with music and dancing. How the father acts toward the older son is also a bit hard to imagine: he does not wait for him to come back from the field where he is working on behalf of the family, nor does he ask his opinion about how to act toward the younger brother. This parable that reveals God's human face the most depicts it as enormously, not defectively, human; humaneness is not lacking in God, and is excessive!

In contrast to the father who compassionately violates the law of just rewards, the two brothers do not succeed in understanding the logic of giving to receive. The younger son receives the part of the inheritance that is due to him, squanders it on prostitutes, and decides to return home when he is at the end of his rope. The younger son does not initially return to his father because he is repentant, but because he has no other way out. In such a situation the most he could imagine is that he might be treated like one of the many hired servants in his father's house. It is not repentance that initially motivates him but hunger!

The older son is likewise thinking only in terms of people getting what they deserve. He has served his father for years, he has never transgressed any of his commands, and he was expecting to be given at least a goat for a feast with his friends. In seeing the father's compassion, the older son accuses him of having violated the principle of just rewards. He does not succeed in thinking about his brother as the son of the same father but defines him only as "this son of yours" (v. 30). Seeing his father only from the perspective of "just rewards" blocks him from recognizing the father as his father and the younger son as his own brother.

Some commentators note the absence of a maternal figure in the parable. However, since the story line concerns the distribution of the family inheritance, that right and duty is the purview of the father, not the mother. In his Letter to the Galatians, Paul states that the proceeds of the sons' inheritance is left up to the father who determines its partitioning when and how he wishes (see 4:1-2). Let us look more closely at the extreme compassion of the father in relation to his sons.

2. The Father Leaves the House Twice

Among the multiple and diverse conflicts that can occur within domestic walls, it is difficult, if not impossible, in some cultures to imagine a father who leaves his place at home to reach out to a son who has deliberately left no trace. If the usual title of "the prodigal son" proposed for the parable is inadequate, it is because the undisputed protagonist is the father who, in the way he relates to both his sons, violates the standard procedure for fair remuneration.

At the beginning of the story, the father grants the request of the younger son. No explanation is offered for why the son asks for his share of the inheritance. Is it because he is in conflict with the older son? Or because he does not share his father's lifestyle? Or because he felt the need to have an independent life? Whatever his motivation, it is not disclosed, since the narrator is interested in the son's hurried departure from his father's house rather than the reason for it.

After a description of the son's dissolute life, the scene returns to the father who acts in astonishing ways. He sees his son from afar, which indicates that he has been waiting for him ever since he left home; he experiences compassion; he runs to meet him; and he embraces and kisses him (v. 20). It leaves the son little time to communicate what he had prepared to say in view of their meeting. The father interrupts him before hearing the son's request to be treated like a hired servant and commands his servants to bring out the best robe, to put a ring on his finger and sandals on his feet, and to kill the fatted calf for a feast. Among all the things the father does for the younger son, the decisive one, which indicates the turning point of the parable, is condensed in the phrase he "had compassion" (v. 20).

The father viscerally loves the lost son with the deepest of human passions. We saw the same phrase as the turning point of the parable of the good Samaritan: "he had compassion" (Lk 10:33). The compassion of the good Samaritan for the dying man is similar to the father's compassion for his lost son. Without compassion it is impossible to run to meet a son, embrace him, and restore his lost dignity. St. John Paul II said it well in his encyclical *Dives in Misericordia*, where he discusses this parable: "The Father's fidelity to himself is totally concentrated upon the humanity of the lost son, upon his dignity" (6). The father's mercy, not his moral virtue, is at the center of the parable. His virtues are good character qualities, but mercy is an orientation that matures in the depths of one's soul and is manifested in actions toward one's neighbor.

His hardest test as a father is still to come. It occurs when the older brother's way of thinking is exposed. The refusal of the older son to enter the house is dramatic; anger transfixes him at the very entrance he had crossed numerous times. So the father decides to go out of the house again to plead with him. This time the price is higher than the price paid for the younger son because the father has to undergo a rebuke that rips him apart! The older son accuses him of being stingy, of not being ready to give him a goat for a feast with his friends. A father seems to have failed in his role when he does not repay the son who is faithful to him but has the fatted calf killed for the son who had squandered his means. Anger leads the older son to distort the truth that he has known from the beginning: the father offered no resistance to the younger son's request for his portion of the inheritance, and the major part of the family inheritance still belongs to the older son.

The father's mercy is unlimited. He could have responded that he was in charge as long as the son lived in his house. According to the rules of inheritance, he could do whatever he wanted with his goods since he was still alive! Instead, the father meets the older son on his level and encourages him to rethink his relationships. The tenderness with which he addresses the older son is immense. Even though the son never calls him "father," he calls him "son" (*teknon*), a word denoting an intimate relationship. The father is aware that the remaining inheritance belongs to his older son, but that is not the issue. Instead, he is preoccupied and focused on wanting to transform "this son of yours" — which is a rebuke by the older son — into "this your brother" (v. 32). The deepest conversion the father is waiting for is not that of the younger son who has come home (initially because he would otherwise have died of hunger); rather it is the conversion of the older son who is incapable of recognizing his father and his brother.

As we think about and speak about "a Church that goes out," we first have to see "the father who goes out" in the parable. Because of his excessive compassion for his two sons, he is not waiting for them inside the house. He runs out to meet the younger one and reaches out to the older one to flood them both with his mercy.

3. The Son Who Died Is Alive

The drama of the younger son is that the more he distances himself from his father, the more his situation deteriorates. After receiving his part of the inheritance, the son goes to a faraway region where he wastes his inheritance and lives a dissolute life. Since there is a herd of pigs in that faraway region, it means that he has gone beyond the borders of the holy land where raising pigs is not permitted because they are considered unclean. Therefore, taking care of pigs is the lowest level of humiliation for the younger son — to the point that he is not even given any pods fed to the swine. When St. Augustine of Hippo assesses his life before conversion, he echoes the condition of the younger son: "At the time of my adolescence I strayed far away from you, and I wandered, my God. I became myself a land of misery" (*Confessions*, 2, 10, 18).

His destitute condition leads the younger son to come to his senses and to reflect on the situation in which he is trapped. He thinks with longing about the servants in his father's house: While he cannot nourish himself even with pods, they have bread in abundance. So he decides to go back home and ask his father to be treated like one of his hired servants to avoid dying of hunger. The younger son also comes to realize he has sinned against heaven and against his father, so he would be satisfied with being treated like a worker. What interests him initially (before he expresses repentance) is to have bread to eat; and since he does not succeed in finding any other solution, he starts walking home.

The embarrassment the son feels as he faces the father who

runs to meet him, embrace him, and kiss him must be enormous. The compassion of the father is undeserved, capable not only of satisfying the son's hunger, but also of restoring his lost dignity. In all haste, without any request for explanations or counting the cost, the father has the son clothed in the best robe and has a ring put on his finger and sandals on his feet. Before seeing his father again, this son was reduced to being a beggar; he no longer had the dignity of a son, but the indignity of caring for unclean animals that were forbidden to be eaten.

The sound of music and dancing coming from the father's house means the father has welcomed his son back into the family; he was dead and is alive; he was lost and has been found. What gives life back to the son who was dead is not repentance by itself but the enormous compassion of the father, compassion for a son who is a new creature and is beginning a new life. The father's compassion is more than just an emotion; it becomes transformed into a passion capable of birthing new life where there was death.

4. "This your brother" (v. 32)

This is just one case, but in sacred Scripture firstborn or older sons do not always have a good lot in life. Although they are destined to be sons of the promise or of inheritance, they often experience the misfortune of people who are deprived of their most natural rights. We know about Cain and Abel, Esau and Jacob, the sons of Jacob vs. Joseph, right up to the sons of Jesse with respect to King David. The enormous paradox of the history of salvation is that the divine law of the firstborn is broken by God himself, and for a very important reason. When it comes to divine remuneration and inheritance, everything must transpire on the level of grace and not on the level of legal rights. In this parable the merciful father recognizes that the patrimony belongs to the older son, but he asks him to adjust his thinking.

The second part of the story becomes a "parable in the parable," and the older son is its protagonist. Returning from the field where

he is working on behalf of his father, he hears the music and dancing, so he asks a servant and is told what is happening. The servant
must have thrown gas on the fire because, with a good dose of irony,
he tells him that the younger brother has returned and his father
has killed the fatted calf.

The older son's fury is uncontrollable. He decides not to enter
the house, and when the father comes outside to plead with him,
he rails against everybody. He accuses the father of being a miser
because he did not give him even a goat, and accuses his younger
brother of being a degenerate who squandered his portion of the
inheritance on prostitutes. At the center of this "parable-in-the-
parable" we find the verb "was angry" (v. 28), which expresses the
exact opposite of the central verb phrase in the first part. While the
father "had compassion" (v. 20) and was viscerally moved for his lost
son, the older brother "was angry" with his father. His rage blinds
him and prevents him from seeing the good: his brother is well; he
was dead, but now he is alive; he was lost, but now he is found. He
can see nothing but the sin committed by his brother, which also
blocks him from seeing the good that the father has kept aside for
him. The wrongdoing of the younger son, which the father does not
hold against him, is blurred out by the brother. It is only from the
older brother that we hear the younger one had spent his inheritance
on prostitutes. The older brother here sounds like the author of the
Book of Sirach who advises, "Do not give yourself to harlots / lest
you lose your inheritance" (9:6).

The parable does not recount either a happy or a sad conclusion
concerning the older brother's ultimate choice. Was he convinced
by the father to enter the house? Did he too decide to ask for his
own inheritance and leave his father's house? Did he ever meet his
younger brother's gaze? The parable of the merciful father is an open
parable that defers the responsibility for appropriate choices to the
listeners. Will they establish relationships according to the standard of legal rights and remunerative justice? Or will they follow
the meandering path of grace and mercy? If they choose the latter

option, people cannot consider the father ungrateful if he applies mercy to a sinner; they need to rejoice when a sinner who was dead comes back to life.

The parables of the sheep and the drachma end on a positive note, while the parable of the merciful father ends in silence. Those who criticize Jesus for welcoming publicans and sinners and eating with them are given the responsibility to choose how to think about their relationship with God (represented by the father) and with their neighbor (represented by the younger brother).

5. Servants, Not Judges, of Mercy

A work of art can be examined from various angles, and each time new and different meanings will emerge. Few commentators of this parable stop to look at the role of the servants more closely because they are considered part of the background. However, there is actually significant tension concerning the servants in the two parts of the parable. On the one hand, the servants participate in the festive reunion of the father and the younger son, and on the other hand, one of them communicates the family news in a negative way to the older son who has just come in from the field.

The servants who participate in the encounter of the father and the younger son carry out the orders they are given: they bring out the best robe; they dress him; they put a ring on his finger and sandals on his feet; they kill the fatted calf and take part in the feast. The servants are also aware of the main reason for the father's many actions: the son who was dead is alive again. The servants are participating in acts of mercy, and there is no objection whatsoever to the enormous compassion of the father. They have their job to do; they clothe the younger son with his lost dignity and organize the feast. It is significant that the father does not clothe his son with his lost dignity by himself but involves his servants in sharing his mercy.

In the second part, one of the servants is questioned by the older son and only says, "Your brother has come, and your father has killed the fatted calf, because he has received him safe and sound" (Lk 15:27). There is a marked contrast between the servants in the first part of the parable and the servant in the second part who reduces his master's mercy to an injustice against the older brother. This servant limits the information he gives to the killing of the calf and his brother's physical health. He does not mention the father's compassion for the son or the other activities he has taken part in except for the killing of the calf. He too is reasoning according to the logic of rewards based on merit and not on grace. The servant knows well that while the best calf is being killed for the younger son, the older son has not received a goat to celebrate with his friends. In other words, the servant seems to be saying to the older brother: "Look at the kind of father you have! Your faithful obedience is worth less than a goat while your brother's dissolution is worth the best calf." And it is the news about the calf that triggers the wrath of the older brother.

In his boundless mercy the father is alone with his older son who, along the line of the servant's viewpoint, minimizes his compassion by reducing it to the level of remuneration. In the relationship of mercy between the father and his two sons, the servants play contrasting roles. They are either servants of mercy for the restoration of the son's lost dignity and share in the joy of their master, or they judge as unjust the extreme compassion of the father for the son that was found.

6. Going from Parables to Real Life: The Encounter with Zacchaeus

The so-called three parables of mercy do not need to be interpreted and instead portray every person's life. They give meaning to existence and lead people to consider life in new ways. At first sight there is a gap to fill between the Jesus who defiles himself by eating with sinners and the protagonists of the three parables. The good shepherd, the housewife, and the merciful father obviously refer to God's compassion. How exactly does Jesus fit in if only God has the right to forgive sins?

The encounter with Zacchaeus (see Lk 19:1-10) bridges the gap between God's way of acting and Jesus' manner, so let us look at how it works. The encounter is described in stages. A crowd gathers to welcome Jesus at the gates of Jericho while he is on his way to Jerusalem. Zacchaeus is a man who has become wealthy by being a tax collector, a profession that was considered unclean. Because of his short stature he cannot see Jesus, so he climbs up a sycamore tree, and Jesus notices him and invites himself to Zacchaeus' house. The tax collector welcomes him joyfully, but the people grumble against Jesus. Zacchaeus publicly promises to give half of his goods to the poor and to restore fourfold what he has stolen.

The turning point is in Jesus' declaration, "Zacchaeus, make haste and come down; for I must stay at your house today" (Lk 19:5). The verb "must" refers not to what Jesus wants from Zacchaeus but to God's will that is about to be realized. We could say it this way: "it is a *must* for God." The strongest link between the parable of the merciful father and the Jesus who eats with sinners occurs through this verb. The father's statement in the parable that it was right "to make merry and be glad" (Lk 15:32) for the return of his lost son, now becomes "I must" in this meeting with Zacchaeus.

God's will is accomplished every time Jesus recognizes the urgency of mercy for sinners. It is the will of God that salvation comes to Zacchaeus. Such a salvation cannot be postponed but happens now. Jesus' statement, "I must stay at your house today," parallels the statement, "Today salvation has come to this house, since he also is a son of Abraham" (Lk 19:9). To meet Jesus is to see the merciful face of God who is always thinking about the salvation of sinners, a salvation that occurs in the present at the time of the encounter. Right up to his last breath Jesus is bringing salvation to a sinner. When the thief on the cross asks Jesus to remember him, Jesus assures him, "Truly, I say to you, today you will be with me in Paradise" (Lk 23:43).

One sentence can summarize the mercy of God that permeates the life of Jesus: "The Son of man came to seek and to save the lost"

(Lk 19:10). Jesus has saved the lost sheep, has found the missing coin, and has gone forth to seek the lost sons and daughters. God's love for sinners motivates this action among human beings as well. It is expressed in great depth by Fyodor Dostoevsky in *The Brothers Karamazov*, when he has the Russian monk Zosima say, "Brothers, have no fear of men's sins. Love a man even in his sin, for that is the semblance of Divine Love and is the highest love on earth."[5]

---

5. Fyodor Dostoevsky, *The Brothers Karamazov*, trans. Constance Garnett (Mineola, NY: Dover Publications, 2005), 270.

CHAPTER SIX

The Opposite of Mercy

The Rich Man and the Beggar Lazarus
Luke 16:19-31

Something valuable is appreciated more when it is missing or if it is replaced by its opposite. And since good is often silenced by evil, at times we need to examine evil to understand and recognize the good. How and when do we esteem mercy? To what point is it possible to trust in the mercy of God? The echo of the three parables of mercy in Luke 15 is still strong, but in this parable there is an enormous obstacle to confront: Which rich people can be saved? And how are they saved?

Shortly before telling this parable, Jesus pronounces a scathing indictment against some Pharisees "who were lovers of money . . . and they scoffed at him" (Lk 16:14). Jesus tells them, "You are those who justify yourselves before men, but God knows your hearts; for what is exalted among men is an abomination in the sight of God" (Lk 16:15). The ensuing parable of the rich man and Lazarus challenges the assumption that if people are exalted before men because of their social status, they are exalted before God as well. But God looks at the heart and not at appearances!

"There was a rich man, who was clothed in purple and fine linen and who feasted sumptuously every day. And at his gate lay a poor man named Lazarus, full of sores, who desired to be fed with what fell from the rich man's table; moreover the dogs came and licked his sores. The poor man died and was carried by the angels to Abraham's bosom. The rich man also died and was buried; and in Hades, being in torment, he lifted up his eyes, and saw Abraham far off and Lazarus in his bosom. And he called out, 'Father Abraham, have mercy upon me, and send Lazarus to dip the end of his finger in water and cool my tongue; for I am in anguish in this flame.' But Abraham said, 'Son, remember that you in your lifetime received your good things, and Lazarus in like manner evil things; but now he is comforted here, and you are in anguish. And besides all this, between us and you a great chasm has been fixed, in order that those who would pass from here to you may not be able, and none may cross from there to us.' And he said, 'Then I beg you, father, to send him to my father's house, for I have five brothers, so that he may warn them, lest they also come into this place of torment.' But Abraham said, 'They have Moses and the prophets; let them hear them.' And he said, 'No, father Abraham; but if some one goes to them from the dead, they will repent.' He said to him, 'If they do not hear Moses and the prophets, neither will they be convinced if some one should rise from the dead.'" (Lk 16:19-31)

1. The Opposite of Mercy

The parable of the rich man and the poor man Lazarus is on the same trajectory as the parables of the good Samaritan and the merciful father. Nevertheless, it presents a contrasting canvas with respect to the two preceding scenes. The story begins similarly to the other two parables: "There was a man . . ." (compare Lk 10:30; 15:11; 16:19). And this time as well there are two episodes: first, the rich man and Lazarus in this world, and second, the rich man, Abraham, and Lazarus in the next world.

In the first scene, a rich man dressed like a king who feasts every day is contrasted to the beggar Lazarus. The rich man wears expensive clothes. The deep red color of the purple dye for his outer clothing is produced by the glands of a mollusk, and that dye was reserved for the clothing of kings and nobles. (Before being crucified, Jesus is clothed in purple to be mocked by the soldiers in the praetorium [see Mk 15:19-20].) The rich man's fine linen is a type of delicate white linen for the garment worn next to his skin. These initial details are enough to make us aware that something is not adding up here. The rich man is clothed as a ruler, but his name is not recorded; the poor man covered with sores has a name, and it is the only name recorded in all of Jesus' parables. He is called Lazarus, which means, "God has helped." (The New Testament also speaks of a Lazarus who is Jesus' friend and the brother of Martha and Mary [see Jn 11:1-2], whom Jesus brings back to life, but that Lazarus has nothing to do with this parable.)

Lazarus lies near the large entrance of the rich man's house, and when he dies he is carried to Abraham's bosom. Some traditions hold that the name of the rich man is *epulone* ("glutton"), but that is not a proper name, and that word is not found in the parable. The law of "counterpoint," or *contrapasso*, is already being set in motion since the rich man, clothed like a king, is destined to anonymity while the poor man has a name that is recorded for eternity.

The two episodes that comprise the parable are disproportionate. While the event involving the two protagonists on earth is allocated a few brushstrokes (see vv. 19-21), the episode in the afterlife, in which the rich man pleads for mercy, is much longer (vv. 22-31), and on one level it will never end. The two scenes are in contrast following the law of reversal. During his earthly life the rich man feasted every day while not even the leftovers from his table were given to Lazarus. In the next life Lazarus is comforted while the rich man does not have even a drop of water to wet his lips. The good things received by the rich man and denied to Lazarus on earth are now reversed: Lazarus is consoled and the rich man is tormented.

Similar to the parables that deal with mercy positively, this one also has a reversal of the situation, but with a difference. The reversal is definitive since there are two obstacles here that are permanent. The first obstacle is the large gate to the house that blocked Lazarus from being helped (which represents the rich man's orientation to the poor). The second obstacle is the abyss that exists in the underworld between where the rich man finds himself and the bosom of Abraham where Lazarus is welcomed.

The disproportion between the situations that transpire in time and in eternity is partially communicated by silence in the dimension of time and by dialogue in the dimension of eternity. Both men's requests remain unsatisfied. In the dimension of time the rich man did not satisfy the hunger of Lazarus, and now, in eternity, Abraham cannot satisfy the rich man's three requests. Lazarus cannot even lift a finger to alleviate the suffering of the rich man. He cannot be sent back to the world to testify about what happens in the afterlife, since not even the resurrection of a dead person can convert the rich man's five brothers.

2. Mercy Not Granted

The contrast between the parables of mercy and the parable of the rich man and Lazarus is enormous. Up until this point, every request for compassion and mercy has been granted, from the total forgiveness of the two debtors by the creditor to the supplication of the prodigal son. In the parables that follow this one, requests are granted to the persistent widow (see Lk 18:1-8) and to the tax collector in the Temple (Lk 18:9-14). The rich man's request in the nether regions — "Have mercy upon me" (Lk 16:24) — is very similar to that of the tax collector in the upcoming parable who says,

"God, be merciful to me a sinner!" (Lk 18:13). However, this is the only case in which a person's supplication is not heard, because the situation is irreversible.

How can any situation be irreversible given the infinite mercy of God? If persevering prayer is capable of affecting God's heart — as we will see with the parable of the persistent widow — then why is the rich man's prayer not able to modify his condition one iota? We are led to understand that his situation has become irreparable because there is no time in eternity. That is the answer that is the most logical, but it is not stated in the parable.

The turning point explains the principal reason why the rich man's situation cannot be resolved. When the rich man is in Hades and sees Lazarus in Abraham's bosom, he recognizes him and calls him by name twice. He thus condemns himself through his own words. He knew exactly who Lazarus was during his earthly life, but he had always ignored him. With great narrative artistry the climax is linked by contrast to the two preceding parables of mercy. In the case of the good Samaritan, "when he saw him, he had compassion" (Lk 10:33), and that is repeated in the merciful father's case: "while he was yet at a distance, his father saw him and had compassion" (Lk 15:20). But now the rich man "lifted up his eyes, and saw Abraham far off and Lazarus in his bosom" (Lk 16:23). The passage does not say "sees him," as in many translations, but "saw him." The rich man is constrained to see in an eternal present the Lazarus he had not paid attention to in the past on earth.

The situation is therefore irremediable because compassion is possible while the poor man lies covered in sores at the rich man's gate; later, compassion makes no sense and is in fact impossible for the rich man. The mercy of God always decreases when mercy for one's neighbor decreases. And when mercy for one's neighbor is lacking, there is no room for God's mercy. It is not by accident that God is never mentioned in the whole parable, because he speaks and acts through Abraham.

Nevertheless, this parable on the opposite of mercy shows the listeners how not to fall into the situation of the rich man — that is, by paying attention now to Moses and the Prophets, the Word of God. The resurrection of a dead person is not enough to convert the rich man's brothers, but how one treats the poor of the world is the litmus test for the path to salvation or to condemnation for any rich person. The poor man the world ignored is acknowledged by the rich man for all eternity!

3. "I Was Hungry and You Gave Me No Food" (Mt 25:42)

The parables that focus on life after death are not told to terrorize the hearers or to describe — as Dante Alighieri does in *The Divine Comedy* — hell, purgatory, and paradise. Instead, in these parables about the end of human life, Jesus speaks about eternity in the context of time, about the future through the present. He is interested in "today" and brings the future into play to challenge his contemporaries. In terms of disavowing or acknowledging the poor, the parable of the rich man and the poor man Lazarus has an enormous bearing on what people should do with their allotted time in this life.

In the contrast between not acknowledging the poor man lying outside the gate of his palace and acknowledging him in eternity, this parable is in line with the parable of the Last Judgment in the Gospel of Matthew 25:31-46. If, in the first part of that parable, the Son of Man blesses and welcomes people who do not know him but who have given food to the hungry and drink to the thirsty, and who have welcomed the stranger, clothed the naked, and visited the sick and those in prison, the second part of the parable is implacable toward the people who have neglected these corporal and spiritual works of mercy. The parable concludes with the criterion that separates the sheep and the goats (those who are blessed and those who are cursed) and is applicable to everybody: "Truly, I say to you, as you did it not to one of the least of these, you did it not to me" (Mt 25:45).

What is said in general about the people who are neglected in

Matthew's parable applies to the parable of the rich man and the beggar Lazarus. Lazarus is hungry, but the rich man does not give him even the leftovers from his table; he is sick and full of sores, but the rich man did not visit him; he is naked, but the rich man did not clothe him; he is a pilgrim who has come to the front door, but the rich man did not show him hospitality. The works of mercy listed in the parable of the Last Judgment were not done for Lazarus whom the rich man ignored during his life, so now he is forced to recognize him forever.

Certain qualifications need to be made about wealth and poverty as reflected in the parable; otherwise, one could fall into simplistic distinctions that are mistaken. By design, the parable does not explain the rationale for Lazarus being carried to Abraham's bosom and the rich man being sent to the nether regions. The story thus avoids considering the poor man blessed *because* he is poor and the rich man cursed *because* he is rich. We have observed that the turning point of the parable is based on the recognition the rich man is forced to give Lazarus. It is not wealth or poverty that guarantees or excludes a positive or negative outcome in the Last Judgment but the ability or inability to see and feel compassion for the other. On this point the drama of the rich man and poor Lazarus hits the mark wherever and whenever it is read. The rich man ignored the poor man during his time on earth, so now he is constrained to acknowledge him for all eternity when any kind of compassion is now useless.

4. Moses, the Prophets, and the Human Heart

Why would Moses and the Prophets be more convincing than the return of a dead man from the afterlife? Or why is the Word of God the only thing able to convert the human heart to compassion? Throughout Luke's Gospel we see two main reasons for this.

First and foremost, mercy flows from the human heart, and only the Word of God is capable of supplying it and preventing it from drying up. The meeting between the Risen One and the disciples at Emmaus is illuminating on this point. In the first part of Luke's narration, "Beginning with Moses and all the prophets, he interpreted to them in all the Scriptures the things concerning himself" (Lk 24:27). After having recognized the Risen One in the breaking of the bread, the disciples confess, "'Did not our hearts burn within us while he talked to us on the road, while he opened to us the Scriptures?'" (Lk 24:32). When the Word of God penetrates the human heart, it is capable of rekindling it and healing it of every kind of blindness and deafness. It makes people capable of seeing what they would not have seen before. The rich man in the parable has an erroneous idea of conversion; he thinks it depends on a miracle like raising someone from the dead. He is unaware that conversion is birthed in hearing the Word of God and not through a dead man coming back to life.

The verb Abraham uses twice concerning Moses and the Prophets in his dialogue with the rich man is decisive: "let them *hear* [Moses and the prophets]. . . . If they do not *hear* Moses and the prophets" (Lk 16:29-31). As long as sacred Scripture remains merely a collection of books to read, it is incapable of opening the eyes of the human heart. The rich man, who is a son of Abraham, calls out to him many times in the underworld: "Father Abraham . . . father . . . father Abraham" (see Lk 16:24, 27, 30). The rich man should know the Bible inside out. However, he has read it but not heard it; if he studied it, he did not receive it into his heart. That is why he tells Abraham that Lazarus needs to be sent back to earth to convert his five brothers. It is not Scripture that is read and studied but Scripture that is *heard* as the Word of God that is capable of converting the human heart and opening it to faith.

The rich man in the parable, who knows Scripture like all the sons of Abraham, is like the rich nobleman that Jesus will encounter shortly after telling this parable (see Lk 18:18-23). The man asks Jesus what he must do to inherit eternal life. He knows the Scriptures and has observed all the commandments since his youth. What he is lacking is the definitive choice to sell what he owns, give it to the poor, and follow Jesus. The nobleman goes away sad because he is too rich; any ensuing action of his would need to be born from the Word heard with his heart. In order for the Word to dwell in a heart there needs to be space in it that is not devoted to riches. In "transcending the literal sense" of Scripture in the Word of God, as Pope Benedict XVI refers to it in *Verbum Domini* (see 38), the action of the Spirit of the Risen One is necessary. Otherwise, Scripture remains a collection of books and is not transformed into the living Word. One of the last actions of the Risen One is that "he opened their minds to understand the Scriptures" (Lk 24:45).

The other reason the Word of God is able to convert the human heart is found in its relationship to the poor. If it is useless for Lazarus to return from the afterlife to convince the rich man's brothers, it is because poor people are at the center of the Gospel. When someone ignores or devalues this essential component of the Gospel, it is useless for a dead man to return to life; the dead man would look just like another "poor Lazarus" but with a different name, so the problem of ignoring him would remain.

This scene, which is fundamental to the entire Gospel of Luke, illustrates the profound relationship between the poor and the Word of God, in this case Moses and the Prophets. At the beginning of his ministry Jesus goes to the synagogue in Nazareth. When he is given the scroll of Isaiah, he opens it and reads from the beginning of Isaiah 61, as recorded in Luke 4:18-19:

> "The Spirit of the Lord is upon me,
> because he has anointed me to preach good news to the poor.
> He has sent me to proclaim release to the captives
> and recovering of sight to the blind,
> to set at liberty those who are oppressed,
> to proclaim the acceptable year of the Lord."

The poor are not left out, nor do they merely have a secondary role. Instead they are at the center of the Gospel. The parable of the

rich man and Lazarus is surprising for its enormous attention on
the rich man. There are no reasons given as to why Lazarus is taken
to Abraham's bosom, and Lazarus never even speaks in the parable.
Instead, the focus is the fate of the rich man. Since he ignored Lazarus during the time he was given on earth, he is forced for eternity
in Hades to acknowledge him, registering his own condemnation.
In this regard, Pope Francis is very clear in *Evangelii Gaudium* that
"the entire history of our redemption is marked by the presence of
the poor" (197).

The question of mercy is a serious question that runs two major
risks in our time: (1) since the mercy of God is infinite, people
will be saved somehow, even if they judged and condemned their
neighbor in the name of God; (2) while divine mercy is assumed to
be an established right, mercy for one's neighbor depends entirely
on everyone's voluntary decision.

However, none of the parables of mercy leads to these conclusions. Mercy always travels in three dimensions (God, I, and the
other) and never just in one dimension (I myself) or in two dimensions (God and I). The dramatic reality of the parable illuminates
mercy by its very opposite. So what is hell? And how can its existence be reconciled with the mercy of God? The same question is
asked by Dostoevsky in *The Brothers Karamzov*, and he comments
on this parable in a surprising way:

> "Fathers and teachers, I ponder, 'What is hell?' I main-
> tain that it is the suffering of being unable to love. Once
> in infinite existence, immeasurable in time and space, a
> spiritual creature was given on his coming to earth, the
> power of saying, 'I am and I love.' Once, once only, there
> was given to him a moment of active *living* love, and for
> that was earthly life given him, and with it times and
> seasons. And that happy creature rejected the priceless
> gift, prized it and loved it not, scorned it and remained
> callous. Such a one, having left the earth, sees Abra-

ham's bosom and talks with Abraham as we are told in the parable of the rich man and Lazarus, and beholds heaven and can go up to the Lord. But that is just his torment, to rise up to the Lord without ever having loved, to be brought close to those who have loved him when he has despised their love."[6] (emphasis in original)

If hell is the suffering of no longer being able to love, every instant of human life that is not lived for love is an anticipation of hell.

---

6. Dostoevsky, *The Brothers Karamazov*, p. 273.

CHAPTER SEVEN

How Do We Change God's Mind?

The Judge and the Widow
Luke 18:1-8

In what circumstances of life do we experience God's mercy the most? When it is needed more than God's other gifts? And how do we recognize it? The Jesus of Luke's Gospel seems to have no hesitation about the answer: the merciful face of God, which shines forth on human life, is seen in prayer. Let us pause, therefore, on this parable dedicated to persistence in prayer, which Jesus tells near the end of his journey to Jerusalem.

> And he told them a parable, to the effect that they ought always to pray and not lose heart. He said, "In a certain city there was a judge who neither feared God nor regarded man; and there was a widow in that city who kept coming to him and saying, 'Vindicate me against my adversary.' For a while he refused; but afterward he said to himself, 'Though I neither fear God nor regard man, yet because this widow bothers me, I will vindicate her, or she will wear me out by her continual coming.'"

And the Lord said, "Hear what the unrighteous judge says. And will not God vindicate his elect, who cry to him day and night? Will he delay long over them? I tell you, he will vindicate them speedily. Nevertheless, when the Son of man comes, will he find faith on earth?" (Lk 18:1-8)

1. A Judge, God, and a Widow

The protagonists in this parable are a judge who does not fear God and a widow. The relationships between the protagonists are again triangular: the judge who is indirectly related to God and directly to a widow. This new relationship is original because in all the other parables we have examined up to this point, God never directly comes into play. He is generally present through a vicarious person (like Abraham in the parable of the rich man and Lazarus), or he is hidden behind someone else (like the merciful father). The selection of characters here is due to the theme of prayer that inspired the parable. In the next chapter on the parable of the Pharisee and the tax collector, God indirectly comes into play because of the same theme of prayer.

According to the social hierarchy during Jesus' time, the judge is a symbol of maximum power, especially in an environment characterized by people's illiteracy and scant familiarity with the law. The judge was like the mayor of a city: lawyer, public prosecutor, and notary. He had unlimited power. At the other end of the scale there is a widow whose status, together with the status of orphans, represents the most precarious of human conditions. When she was not able to rely on the familial and civil authority of her husband, a widow was often forced to suffer various abuses. The height of power and the lowest point of powerlessness are juxtaposed here. Along with the two protagonists, God is also the focus of attention since the judge involves God indirectly at the beginning. We are told that the judge does not fear God, and then he admits it himself; at the end there is a comparison between the judge and God.

Jesus emphasizes in a special way the gulf between the civil power of the judge and the widow's situation. The judge has no fear of God and is not a religious person. In addition to not fearing or believing in the God of Israel, he renders judgment according to his own pleasure! More than being a dishonest judge, he is an unjust judge who lacks a compassionate heart because he does not believe in God.

On the opposite side of the spectrum is the widow who calls on the judge persistently for justice against her adversary. The parable tells us nothing about her adversary. What is of interest here is the judge's arbitrary power as compared to God's in terms of justice and the insistence of the widow. After several pleadings, the judge decides to grant the widow's request. However, it is not compassion that changes his mind but the continual persistence of the widow.

2. God Is Not a Judge

After telling the parable of the judge and the widow, Jesus turns to the listeners and asks them what they generally think about God's action. Having recourse to an *a fortiori* argumentation that proceeds from a minor proposition to a major proposition, Jesus asks his listeners if God will render better justice for his chosen ones and do so more quickly than the judge did for the widow. Unlike the unjust judge, God will do justice quickly for his elect who cry out to him day and night.

Despite the enormous difference between the judge and God, there is one characteristic they have in common that illustrates the inestimable value of prayer. Both of them revise their approach to the widow and to the elect based on the supplications they receive. People often think that God is someone who is immovable and does not change his plans for human beings. The West has become accustomed to thinking of a God without passion who does not let himself be affected by any external agents. However, the history of salvation conveys a very different picture of God. He is a God who lets himself be petitioned by people about their situations and who listens to the prayers of his elect (the poor and the weak) who are beseeching him.

As for God's openness to revise his plans, we see two representative episodes in the Old Testament: the prayer of King Hezekiah and the repentance of the inhabitants of Nineveh. The Second Book of Kings recounts that Hezekiah became gravely ill and his life was hanging by a thread. He turned his face to the wall of his house and prayed this prayer: "Remember now, O LORD, I beg you, how I have walked before you in faithfulness and with a whole heart, and have done what is good in your sight" (20:3). The Lord hears Hezekiah's prayer and weeping, and he heals him of his sickness.

The Book of Jonah describes how God changes his mind about the evil he had threatened against the inhabitants of Nineveh (see 3:10). A merciful God is a difficult concept for Jonah: "That is why I made haste to flee to Tarshish; for I knew that you are a gracious God and merciful, slow to anger, and abounding in mercy, and that you repent of evil" (Jon 4:2). The prophet tried every way he could to prevent the mercy of God for that city, so after preaching to the inhabitants of Nineveh, he stays to see if God will punish them. When the inhabitants of Nineveh are doing penance, Jonah sets himself up east of the city under the shade of a booth. To relieve him, God grows a plant to shade him and give him some comfort, but the next day he withers it, and Jonah asks to die. With an argument that foreshadows our parable, God asks the prophet, "You pity the plant, for which you did not labor, nor did you make it grow, which came into being in a night, and perished in a night. And should not I pity Nineveh . . . ?" (Jon 4:10-11).

The God of the New Testament and the Old Testament is a God who lets his heart be touched because he does not wish for a sinner to die but to be converted and live (see Ez 33:11).

3. What Should We Ask for, and How Do We Pray?

The parable of the judge and the widow concludes with the judge's promise to do justice for the woman because of her persistence.

Persistent prayer is also capable of changing God's heart. Neverthe-less, people often experience unanswered prayer, and feel as though their prayers were never even heard. Where are God's compassion and mercy when the cries of his elect who are the neediest — rang-ing from the widow to the orphan and finally to poor and sick children — do not seem to be heard? And if they are heard, why do the results seem to demonstrate that the requests were not granted? The Jesus of Luke's Gospel is the Master of prayer, and to address this dramatic reality he tells the parable of the persistent friend.

That parable, told earlier in Luke 11:5-8, has some traits in common with the parable of the widow and the judge (although it does not involve the mercy of God). It recounts the story of a man who has nothing to offer his unexpected guests, so he knocks on a neighbor's door to ask him for three loaves of bread. Unfortunately, it is midnight and the neighbor has already locked the door of his house and his children are in bed. Faced with the insistence of his friend at the door, in the end he is forced to get up and give him the bread he requested.

In the explanation that follows in verses 9-13, Jesus exhorts people to ask, seek, and knock because God is capable of giving, finding, and opening. And then he says that if a father is capable of giving his son a fish instead of a serpent and an egg instead of a scorpion, how much more willing God is to give the Holy Spirit to those who ask him. At first glance it does not seem that the Holy Spirit is at issue here in the least! However, he is the principal gift to ask for in prayer because only the Spirit allows us to distinguish a fish from a serpent and an egg from a scorpion. Many times people pray for what seems useful and necessary to them, but it may not seem so to God because what they ask for is secondary and does not enter into his will.

In prayer we do not know what to ask for. This is the occasion in which people experience human weakness more than anywhere else. But it is just in these situations that "the Spirit helps us in our weakness; for we do not know how to pray as we ought, but the

Spirit himself intercedes for us with sighs too deep for words. And he who searches the hearts of men knows what is the mind of the Spirit, because the Spirit intercedes for the saints according to the will of God" (Rom 8:26-27).

It is easy to stop praying when prayer seems to go unanswered. It is difficult to persist like the insistent widow, but God is more willing than any judge to listen quickly to the cry of his chosen ones. Believers are asked to persevere in prayer even when the outcomes are different than what had been hoped for.

4. Persevering in Faith

The parable of the judge and the widow poses a question that we need to ponder. Will Jesus find faith on earth when he returns? We often have an unclear or limited understanding of faith. We think "faith" is identified with a group of concepts, so it is the same for everybody, or, conversely, that it corresponds to what is incomprehensible. Faith is actually difficult to hold onto especially when people ask for something that is not granted; they then desist in prayer and end up with a lack of faith.

The model for the relationship between prayer and faith is what is said about Jesus in the Letter to the Hebrews: "In the days of his flesh, Jesus offered up prayers and supplications, with loud cries and tears, to him who was able to save him from death, and he was heard for his godly fear. Although he was a Son, he learned obedience through what he suffered; and being made perfect he became the source of eternal salvation to all who obey him" (5:7-9). Jesus, in his humanity, went through his time of trial but clung to God's mercy, thereby demonstrating a faith in which he surrendered himself without reservation into the arms of the Father.

What Jesus suffered did not distance him from God, but allowed him to learn a faith that was obedient to the will of the Father. What the Letter to the Hebrews says seems paradoxical, though. How is it possible to say that Jesus' prayer in the garden was heard if he had to drink the whole cup he asked to have removed?

How can we consider his prayer answered if he had to endure the humiliation of the cross? He was indeed heard by the Father, but his prayer was answered with a resurrection that always comes through death on the cross.

The faith requested of those who hear the parable of the judge and the widow simultaneously includes trust, faithfulness, and confidence. It is born of prayer and ends in obedience for those who learn to be guided by God's will even when they do not understand it. Unfortunately, in our time it is increasingly difficult and rare to have steadfastness in prayer and the openness to receive answers that are often different than what we requested.

5. He Saw Him with the Eyes of Mercy, He Chose Him

The parallel between the widow and God's elect needs to be examined more closely because it expresses one of the most disconcerting truths of the Gospel. It is true that God is not on the side of the judge who does not, among other things, have any fear of him but is on the side of the widow. The elect of God are the orphans and the widows who cannot deal, by themselves, with the abuses to which they are subjected. So then, why does Jesus choose people with moral defects and sinners like Levi who is a tax collector? "He went out, and saw a tax collector, named Levi, sitting at the tax office; and he said to him, 'Follow me.' And he left everything, and rose and followed him" (Lk 5:27-28).

In the explanation that follows, Jesus specifies that "those who are well have no need of a physician, but those who are sick ..." and that he did not "come to call the righteous, but sinners to repentance" (see Lk 5:31,32). The logic of election is hard to understand. God chooses those who are weak, despised, and ignoble in the world to confound those who are strong, wise, and noble, so that no one can boast of their rights before him (1 Cor 1:26-29). In positive terms, God chooses the former to reach the latter; otherwise it is inevitable for us to think that his choice would automatically exclude the others. What is said in Exodus 33:19 and repeated by Paul is still valid:

"He says to Moses, 'I will have mercy on whom I have mercy, and I will have compassion on whom I have compassion'" (Rom 9:15). In what sense is God merciful to whomever he chooses? Can he exclude anyone from his mercy? And who are the elect?

God's choice in this matter is filled above all with grace from beginning to end and is not conditioned by any outside agent. God does not choose people because they are good, but to make the people he chooses *become* good. Concerning his own election, Paul explains: "Christ Jesus came into the world to save sinners. And I am the foremost of sinners; but I received mercy for this reason, that in me, as the foremost, Jesus Christ might display his perfect patience" (1 Tm 1:15-16).

People are chosen by grace not in order to exclude others but to include them in God's mercy. Unfortunately, when we think of the elect, we often fall into the trap of exclusivity. In reality God chooses some not in order to reject others but to include everyone. In so doing, the terrible parable of "predestination" does not involve election and rejection but only election. In God's plan there is no predestination to good or evil, but only and always to good. And that choice depends not on God's goodness but on the fact that, as Jesus explains in the dialogue with Nicodemus at night, "God so loved the world that he gave his only-begotten Son, that *whoever* believes in him should not perish but have eternal life" (Jn 3:16, emphasis added). Only when we think of election without standing before the cross of Christ can we imagine that there exists an election of some people to the disadvantage of others or, even worse, against others.

The result of election through God's mercy is not demonstrated through arrogance or presumption, but through service to others. If God is "the Father of mercies and God of all comfort," it is because he "comforts us in all our affliction, so that we may be able to comfort those who are in any affliction, with the comfort with which we ourselves are comforted by God" (2 Cor 1:3-4). However, election does not occur first and then mercy; the mercy of God is transformed into election. Venerable Bede says it well in his commentary about the calling of Levi (or Matthew): "Jesus saw the publican and since he saw him with the eyes of mercy, he chose him and told him, 'Follow me'" (*Homily 21*, 149).

Pope Francis' motto is *Miserando atque eligendo* ("By showing mercy and by choosing").

CHAPTER EIGHT

Who Is Justified by God?

The Pharisee and the Publican in the Temple
Luke 18:9-14

Who is justified before God and how is he justified? The parable of the Pharisee and the publican in the Temple is told to challenge a mistaken appropriation of justification that leads to judging and condemning others. The parable is told soon after the parable on persistent prayer, but now the overview is broader because the question of God's justice toward human beings arises. With great psychological artistry, the Jesus of Luke's Gospel penetrates once again the twists and turns inside the human heart and evaluates the thoughts and sentiments that emerge from within:

> He also told this parable to some who trusted in themselves that they were righteous and despised others: "Two men went up into the temple to pray, one a Pharisee and the other a tax collector. The Pharisee stood and prayed thus with himself, 'God, I thank you that I am not like other men, extortioners, unjust, adulterers, or even like this tax collector. I fast twice a week, I give tithes of all that I get.' But the tax collector, standing far off, would not even lift up his eyes to heaven, but beat his breast,

saying, 'God, be merciful to me a sinner!' I tell you, this man went down to his house justified rather than the other; for every one who exalts himself will be humbled, but he who humbles himself will be exalted." (Lk 18:9-14)

1. A Pharisee and a Publican

The scene takes place in the Temple, where two protagonists who remain anonymous have gone to pray. The two men are chosen not to condemn or praise the two groups they belong to but to convey an idea of the personalities in the parable. The first is not to be considered proud because he belongs to the Pharisee movement, nor is the other to be considered humble because he is a tax collector. It is not their origins that make them justified or sinful, but rather their manner of relating to God and their neighbor.

The Temple in Jerusalem is the setting for this scene. Until the Romans destroyed it in A.D. 70, it was one of the landmarks for Jewish piety and, among other things, it was the place to expiate sins and have them forgiven. As usual, the parable presents a triangular relationship: a Pharisee, a publican, and God whom they are addressing. God as the third person of the triad is important in relation to the two men because both men's prayers begin with "God" (Lk 18:11, 13), and in the end the publican is justified but not the Pharisee (see Lk 18:14).

However, the attitudes and the prayers of the two protagonists are in contrast. Both turn to the same God, but they have opposite ideas and attitudes. The Pharisee prays standing up, while the publican does not even have the courage to lift up his eyes to heaven and is beating his breast. The contents of their prayers are even more contrasting. In the Greek language of this Gospel the Pharisee uses twenty-nine words, while the publican says only six words.

The Pharisee thanks God that he is not like other men who are extortioners, unjust, adulterers, or like the publican who is praying at a proper distance. The irony of the Pharisee's prayer is subtle and piercing. He does not list others to entrust them to the Lord but to despise and condemn them, just like the people to whom Jesus addresses the parable who consider themselves justified and judge others (see Lk 18:9). At the very moment he considers himself sinless, the Pharisee commits one of the most serious sins: he substitutes himself for God in condemning his neighbor. He shamelessly mentions his excessive observance of the law. While according to Leviticus 16:29-31 fasting is obligatory for the Day of Atonement, the Pharisee in the parable fasts twice a week. He follows the diet that forbids eating unclean food — for example, pork — and he pays a tithe on whatever he acquires. He is a perfect example of someone who exalts himself before God.

With a penitential attitude, the publican only says, "God, be merciful to me a sinner!" (Lk 18:13). His prayer expresses the essential in a few words. It contains the recognition of his guilt and a request for mercy so he can receive forgiveness. His penitential prayer is like the one in Psalm 79:9: "Deliver us, and forgive our sins, / for your name's sake!"

2. The Reversal

When it comes time to draw conclusions, Jesus addresses his listeners and highlights the reversal in the situation with a final broad brushstroke: the one who goes home justified is the tax collector, not the Pharisee, since whoever exalts himself will be humbled and whoever humbles himself will be exalted. The One who lifts up the humble and abases the proud is God, as Mary sings in the *Magnificat*: he "has scattered the proud in the imagination of their hearts, / he has put down the mighty from their thrones, / and exalted those of low degree" (Lk 1:51-52). God's way is to remove the powerful from their thrones — especially those like the Pharisee in the parable who need to trample on the dignity of others in order to exalt themselves — and to raise up the humble. The Pharisee's attitude was arrogant; the publican's was humble. Despite his long prayer the Pharisee is not justified, while the tax collector's brief prayer is sufficient for him to go home justified.

What determined the reversal in the situation? Since two representative characters are chosen, the parable is focused around two turning points. In the first part, the turning point in the Pharisee's prayer is that it is not enough for him to exalt himself before God; he also has to compare himself to others and despise them. The focal point occurs in the phrase "or even like this tax collector" (Lk 18:11). The rest of his prayer is not wrong; on the contrary he is a man who is zealous for the law and for Jewish traditions. What sends him home not justified is his disdain for the publican. He judges him, unaware of his repentance and prayer because of the distance that separates the two men in the Temple.

The turning point in the second part is in the tax collector's prayer: "God, be merciful to me a sinner!" (v. 13). The publican does not attempt to add extenuating circumstances such as, "Since my job is considered defiling, I am trying to make only a minor profit," or, "I have a family to support and I cannot change my job." Instead, he presents himself before God with his heart laid bare. In a very short prayer he expresses what is pleasing to God: his acknowledgement of wrongdoing and his hope of forgiveness. Acknowledging oneself as a sinner before God is the necessary condition for being justified; the arrogance of people who think they are sinless does not prevail in this situation.

3. Justification by Grace

Unfortunately, in our time, one of the words that is most prone to ambiguity is "justification." In popular language it is the equivalent of finding a reason that excuses one's guilt. In work environments, people need to "justify" proposed changes. The words "justice" and "reconciliation" have also become ambiguous. "Justice" is often seen as a form of reward in which good is reserved for those who do good and evil for those who do evil. And "reconciliation" is understood as the result of re-established peace between people who were in conflict.

This parable expresses a different vision of justice, justification, and reconciliation. What these three words have in common is reflected in the grace that God concedes to the publican and not the Pharisee. In contrast to the man who justifies himself, the other man waits for grace from the Lord to be justified. Certain qualifications need to be made about this primacy of grace, or the parable could be misunderstood and exploited. Grace does not come as a result of sin. It is a mistake to think that it is necessary to sin in order to obtain justification and reconciliation with God or that the more one sins the more one receives divine grace. If that were the case, our thinking would not be very different from the Pharisee's thinking. It would mean that grace is conditioned by sin (the publican's sin), just the way grace is conditioned by merit (the Pharisee's merit). However, the grace of justification is always freely given and goes far beyond any human action, good or bad.

The concept of the primacy of grace has led to a misunderstanding that it was necessary to do evil or to not observe the law in order to receive the benefit of grace. In his Letter to the Romans, St. Paul reacts against this kind of distortion to emphasize that grace abounds not *because* it is proportionate to sin but because people are justified in Christ only by grace: "Therefore, since we are justified by faith, we have peace with God through our Lord Jesus Christ. Through him we have obtained access to this grace in which we stand" (5:1-2).

A final misunderstanding concerns the way in which justification by God happens. In general, people think that God must first exercise justice and then justify the sinner. The idea is that, in fairness, God first gives people what they deserve and then justifies them. However, this misunderstands a central fact about divine justice, that God is just at the very moment in which he justifies the sinner. The parable sheds light on this fact: justification is accorded to the tax collector, but it does not come after getting what he deserved. If that were the case, the Pharisee would be partly justified because he is a zealous observer of the law. Instead, there is no gap between the justice of God and the justification of the sinner. God is just when he justifies the sinner!

Finally, the principal consequence of justification is significant: reconciliation with God for a new and unexpected relationship. Justification is a free action on God's part, and the tax collector's justification goes beyond any expectation. However, this reconciliation does not correspond to the re-establishment of peace between two people who are on the same level. The whole paradox of reconciliation in Christ is that while in general the one who was wrong has to make amends and ask to be reconciled with the one who was right — "that is, in Christ God was reconciling the world to himself, not counting their trespasses against them, and entrusting to us the message of reconciliation" (2 Cor 5:19). The Pharisee does not go home justified because his good works do not prevent him from judging others while the tax collector, who avoids judging anybody, is justified.

4. The Merciful Justice of God

For centuries this parable has been interpreted as a criticism of the Jewish religion: the Pharisee equals the Jews and the tax collector the Christians. Actually, Jesus intended to set the scene of two contrasting ways of relating to God and neighbor that can happen in any religious sphere, including that of the Church. The risk of considering oneself guiltless and the need to downgrade others to exalt oneself is unfortunately present throughout all of humanity and is not limited to any particular religion.

The bias that considered Judaism to be a religion of merit and Christianity to be a religion of grace seems to have played a determining role in an erroneous reading of this parable. However, that approach risks producing the false picture that the Old Testament presented a different God than the God of Jesus Christ and the early Christian communities. In the Old Testament the justice of God is in fact connected to his salvation and mercy, just as the prophet Hosea states: "I will espouse you for ever; I will espouse you in righteousness and in justice, in steadfast love, and in mercy" (Hos 2:19).

As for the generations of people that follow one another throughout time, Psalm 145:7-8 says:

They shall pour forth the fame of your abundant goodness,
and shall sing aloud of your righteousness.
The LORD is gracious and merciful,
slow to anger and abounding in mercy.

The *Rule of the Community* 11, 11-12 in the Qumran contains a wonderful prayer on God's merciful justice:

As for me, if I stumble
The mercy of God will be my salvation forever;
If I fall into sins of the flesh
My judgment will be according God's justice, which lasts
forever.

We are at an enormous distance from the vision of a God who limits himself to judging people for their sin. Sin is sin, and there is no need ever to confuse it with the good, but the justice of the God is just when it transforms itself into mercy for the remission of sins.

The Old and New Testaments are filled with a justice that reveals the merciful face of God without ever mistaking good for evil, but rather converting evil into good. This parable teaches us that we should let ourselves be reached by the love of Christ. The scandal Jesus provokes for some who think they are justified becomes even more intense through the scandal of the cross: "[God] made him to be sin who knew no sin, so that in him we might become the righteousness of God" (2 Cor 5:21). On the cross, Jesus was made sin so that the righteousness of God could reach everyone, bringing each person into right relationship with himself.

The parable of the Pharisee and the publican sets forth an enormous paradox for everyone. The sinner is justified while the man who presumed on his own righteousness was not. Wherever there is judgment of another, the justice of God disappears.

The Gospel and Mercy in the Parables

Why talk about mercy in so many parables? Aren't the three parables in Luke 15 enough? The truth is that the human heart is a deep abyss and mercy is a serious issue. It is easy to talk about mercy, but difficult to live it! Let us review a few major points in the various parables that touched on the mercy of God toward human beings.

1. The Different Faces of Mercy

Mercy as the forgiveness of a debt that has been incurred (like the sin of human beings) is reflected in the parable of the two debtors forgiven by their creditor (see Lk 7:41-43). Whoever receives a greater pardon is disposed to love more, while he who has little forgiven loves less. The first feature of mercy is that it is a grace that generates gratitude. Gratitude is the dominant reaction for the gratuitous justification of a sinner.

Seen from the angle of compassion for the other, mercy does not have to run around looking for a neighbor to love but finds him in the street, like the dying man who was helped by a Samaritan (see Lk 10:25-37). Love for God is always operative in love for one's neighbor without it needing to be a separate commandment.

Mercy as the search for someone who is lost, as opposed to

those who presume they are safe and secure, is echoed in the parable of the sheep that was lost (see Lk 15:4-7). Such paradoxical mercy is applied for a single sinner who converts because every single person is precious, just as one drachma is precious despite the other nine drachmas the woman has in her house (Lk 15:8-10).

A father moved by enormous compassion leaves his house twice to save his two sons. He runs to the younger son and holds a feast for him and then exits his house to entreat the older son to come join the feast (see Lk 15:11-32).

To acknowledge a poor person like Lazarus only in the afterlife is useless. We need to see him and help him when he is still alive, because where there is no mercy for the other then God's mercy is absent too (see Lk 16:19-31). The salvation of a rich man occurs through helping the poor.

Persevering prayer can bring about mercy when God changes his mind, more than when a persistent widow receives mercy from an unjust judge (see Lk 18:1-8). The chosen of God, the weak and the poor, are in God's thoughts. His election does not exclude other people but begins with the least to reach everyone.

Mercy justifies and restores even a sinner like a tax collector whose occupation is sinful, while God can do nothing for someone who performs righteous works but condemns a sinner in order to exalt himself (see Lk 18:9-14).

We can see that Jesus' attention in Luke's Gospel is focused on the essential traits of mercy rather than on making moral judgments. Mercy occurs through relationships that issue from the human heart and are poured into words and actions.

2. Open-ended Conclusions

If we set aside the parable of the rescued sheep and the recovered drachma that conclude with shared rejoicing, the other parables of mercy conclude in an open-ended manner, leaving listeners with the responsibility to choose wisely. We are not told what Simon the Pharisee does after hearing the parable of the two debtors and their creditor. The lawyer, who hears the parable of the good Samaritan, is invited to become a neighbor to the other and not to decide who his neighbor is as he pleases. Did those who heard the three so-called "parables of mercy" continue or stop murmuring against Jesus? Did the agonizing parable of the rich man and Lazarus convince the rich that they are deluding themselves if they think they will be exalted in the next life the way they were exalted in this life? The parable of the judge and the widow ends with a disquieting question: When the Son of Man returns, will he find faith in the earth? And how many who despise others to exalt themselves will be persuaded to change because of the parable of the Pharisee and the tax collector praying in the Temple?

If the parables of Jesus continue to challenge readers in whatever time and place they live, it means that the parables remain relevant for everyone by representing the reality of life in very authentic ways. A real relationship with God for people in the past, mediated through Jesus' preaching, is the same for people today and will be the same for the people of tomorrow.

The parables of mercy are located at the borders of the Gospel. Without taking anything away from Jesus' preaching about the kingdom of God, the mercy of God moves out through the parables beyond the circle of disciples and dialogues with everyone who hears them. Even if the parables themselves do not bring salvation — which only happens in a personal encounter with Jesus and his death and resurrection — they do explore new pathways, and they travel on inaccessible roads where the Gospel has not yet reached or where it is unheard. Therefore, if it is unthinkable that salvation can come from merely understanding a parable, it is also undeniable that Jesus' parables indicate paths to salvation in remarkable ways.

3. Other Examples of Mercy

The Roman philosopher Seneca advises his friend Lucilius that "the path is long through precepts, but it is short and efficient through examples" (*Epistle* 6, 5). Is there anyone besides Jesus who put into practice the exhortation to be as merciful as our Father? Let us take a brief look at Luke's Gospel and the Acts of the Apostles.

The third Gospel begins with two hymns that both speak of mercy. The first is the canticle of Mary, after the annunciation during her visit to her cousin Elizabeth, known as the *Magnificat*:

> For he who is mighty has done great things for me,   '
> and holy is his name.
> And his mercy is on those who fear him
> from generation to generation.
> He has shown strength with his arm,
> he has scattered the proud in the imagination of their hearts,
> he has put down the mighty from their thrones,
> and exalted those of low degree. (Lk 1:49-52)

What God did in the life of a humble young girl in Galilee anticipates the customary reversal in situations that we find in the parables. In harmony with Mary, Zechariah, the father of John the Baptist, sings his own *Benedictus*. When he finds himself facing the miracle of a long-awaited son, he blesses God who has visited his people:

> To perform the mercy promised to our fathers,
> and to remember his holy covenant,
> the oath which he swore to our father Abraham, to grant us
> that we, being delivered from the hand of our enemies,
> might serve him without fear,
> in holiness and righteousness before him all the days of our life.
> And you, child, will be called the prophet of the Most High;
> for you will go before the Lord to prepare his ways,
> to give knowledge of salvation to his people
> in the forgiveness of their sins,
> through the tender mercy of our God,
> when the day shall dawn upon us from on high. (Lk 1:72-78)

The merciful compassion of God is heartfelt; he is a God who manifests himself not with judgment but with the same compassion the merciful father had for his two sons. "The humble of the land (or of the country)," as they were called in Jesus' time — those who did not belong to any privileged circle — are the examples that Luke first points to in the parables of mercy. Whenever people want to experience God's mercy firsthand, they need to become involved with the humble — in the land, in the Church, and in society — where the overturning of people's situations brings the wonder and joy of mercy.

Another example of mercy occurs in the Acts of the Apostles during the martyrdom of the deacon Stephen: "And as they were stoning Stephen, he prayed, 'Lord Jesus, receive my spirit.' And he knelt down and cried with a loud voice, 'Lord, do not hold this sin against them.' And when he had said this, he fell asleep" (Acts 7:59-60). Stephen's last words recall those of Jesus on the cross on behalf of his executioners: "Father, forgive them; for they know not what they do" (Lk 23:34).

With the necessary qualifications, the martyrdom of Stephen is an authentic imitation of the passion of Christ and reproduces it during the time of the Church. Christian martyrdom is the height of mercy because it parallels Christ's gift of his life for others, without any trace of vengeance or hate, and converts evil into good.